The Ladder of Transpersonal Leadership in the Global Organization

Antonio Nicolás Rubino
Manuela Amat

Houston, Texas
2018

Antonio Nicolás

To the people who have been with me all these years: our journey has been a learning experience. To my mother who taught me how beautiful life is. To my brother who, without knowing it, taught me the value of diversity.

Manuela

To the memory of my parents, examples of love, honesty and perseverance. To my sons, who represent the children of the world, to them I dedicate this small contribution.

Antonio Nicolás y Manuela

To the managers and leaders who, with their ideas and actions, showed us a true sense of transpersonal leadership. They have given us the raw material to build our reflections.

Contents

Introduction

What is leadership? Who are real leaders? Are there differences between leaders and managers? If so, what are they? Are leaders necessarily those who command us? Are there different types of leadership? How do we recognize a real leader from a false one? This book will help you to find the answers.

The Ladder to Transpersonal Leadership includes elements of leadership theories and approaches assembled into a socio-ecological approach, which considers the interaction among processes, people, context, and time. When leaders become transpersonal, they reach a global awareness, thereby moving from local, regional, and organizational contexts to a global context.

The book has eleven parts; in the first part, we review the concepts of leadership and leadership development. We explore some approaches to leadership (attributes, effective leadership approach, and relationships among power, influence, and leadership). We continue with situational leadership and its relation to contextual factors. Finally, we present some of the latest approaches to developing an organizational vision and the role of the leader as a facilitator of development.

In the second part, we explore the fundamentals of transpersonal leadership, and we ask the question: who is a leader?

In the third part, we explore the first step of leadership: influencing people. This step explores the leader's abilities to move people in a previously determined direction. We include different forms of influencing people, some of which include rational persuasion, emotional persuasion, consulting, ingratiation, personal interest, transaction, coalition, legitimation, and pressure. Additionally, we established which tactics are more appropriate from the transpersonal leadership framework.

In the fourth part, "Influencing without Using Low Order Rewards", we provided a qualitative dimension to leadership. We point out that simply exerting influence is not enough to be a leader, but that it is necessary to influence using socially acceptable principles that yield benefits and increase well-being for all followers. In this step, we advocate against using low order rewards, such as gifts or punishments. The leader should center on people and must place a high value on other opinions and viewpoints. We also consider different forms of power used by leaders to influence their followers. We explore the types of power, such as expert, referent, reward, coercive, and legitimate. Additionally, we include the power by possession of information. We analyze the bases of power as related to democracy and participatory processes when setting group goals and objectives.

In the fifth part, "Actively Promoting and Enabling People and Organizational Development", we provide a sense of direction for leaders. When the leaders arrive at this step, they understand that their job is to facilitate the discovery of people's potentialities. Leaders must keep in mind that personal development relates intrinsically to the development of the organization. In this step, the leader centers on the group and on the organization. In this section, we review concepts such as empowerment, shared decision-making, and democracy. Additionally, we develop the concepts of faith, trust, and conviction as they relate to leadership.

In the sixth part, "Developing and Practicing a Socio-Centered Orientation", we discuss the meaning of socio-centered orientation, in which society is the focus of attention and leaders must be sensitive to elements beyond the organizational context. This step has to do with leaders' awareness of their actions and effects on the organization, the community, and the society. In this section, we explore some concepts around organized groups - organizations, communities, and societies. These concepts include prescriptive, entrepreneur, and knowledge organizations and societies. We explore the actions leaders should take on each of these. Furthermore, we establish the need to practice transpersonal leadership in knowledge organizations, a type of organization that uses information and knowledge to solve problems and make decisions.

The seventh part, Practicing a Global and Ecological Orientation, constitutes the leader's highest developmental level. This step has to do with the leader's acquisition of a global awareness. Leaders reach this step when they understand that their actions affect, and are affected by, other people, communities, and cultures. In this section, we explore the fundamental characteristics and behaviors of transpersonal leaders. We also express some thoughts involving leadership actions including taking risks, creating a quality atmosphere in the organization, the society, and the planet, providing opportunities to people so they can access information and use knowledge for their well-being and for empowering people by teaching them how to learn to learn.

In the eighth section, we explore some ideas about ethics and leadership. We begin with the definitions of ethics and ethical systems, and we relate these elements to leaders' decision making. We explore some ethical concepts and mention different ways to practice ethical leadership. We conclude by establishing the relationship between ethics and transpersonal leadership.

In the ninth section, we define Transpersonal leadership as a process through which the leader actively develops and promotes followers' development in order to achieve shared goals that lead to personal, organizational, social and global well-being. In this section, we review some actions that transpersonal leaders must promote and facilitate. These actions include the following:

- Managing their personal growth based on ethical and moral elements
- Facilitating others' development so that they may achieve higher ethical and moral levels
- Leading while bearing in mind their own characteristics, followers' individualities, and contextual factors
- Combining internal and external motivation to achieve individual progress
- Moving from the ego, to the organization, and to the society - using their personal, organizational, social, and global knowledge to provide and promote significant meaning in their collaborators.

In the tenth section, "Final Notes", we present the essential conditions to reach transpersonal leadership. In this section, we leave some questions for you to think about, to help you build your mental models, to construct your own conclusions on leadership, and to define who transpersonal leaders are.

In the eleventh section, we present a short summary of transpersonal leadership in the organizational context, and we establish some differences between managers and leaders within the transpersonal leadership frame of reference.

Previous Considerations

Have the concepts of what are leader and leadership changed? Are there new, significant studies that address leadership? Do we need to understand leadership to talk appropriately about it?

We believe so...

In the following paragraphs, we make a short review of the leadership concept. If you do not wish to read these theoretical considerations, please, feel free to go to The Leadership Ladder, in the proceeding section.

The first the studies on leadership focused on the characteristics of leaders. These studied indicated that leaders were people with special characteristics since birth. Other leadership scholars have proposed that people have personal characteristics, which, after being developed, transformed them into leaders. Perhaps, the idea that leaders are born with certain characteristics is the reason by which many people said that leaders were born; or expressed it in a more common way: "he or she is a born leader type."

This focus of leadership studies eventually shifted to environmental factors that influence leadership effectiveness. Scholars considered that leadership was the product of the interaction between personal characteristics and the environment. In addition, they pointed out that, on many occasions, the environment "pushed" a person to become a leader.

Later, leadership studies included a set of behaviors practiced by people. These behaviors served to categorize a person as a leader.

Recently, leadership studies have examined how leaders create a symbolic focus and a group vision to improve group development and organizational development.

So, from early leadership studies to those of the present day, leadership approaches have included:

- Trait approach.
- Roles and behaviors (effective vs. ineffective) approaches.
- Power and influence processes (between leaders and followers) approaches.

- Situational and Contextual factors (influencing leadership development and leader-follower relationships) approaches.
- Transactional and transformational (leader and followers) approaches.
- Group leadership approaches.

We believe that to understand leadership it is necessary to have a theoretical and practical comprehension of it. Learning about leadership is fundamental to understanding who is a leader, and who is not, and to developing ourselves as leaders. Based on this premise, we present a short review of leadership concepts and their development in social and organizational contexts. We believe that a good reflective exercise is to categorize some of the leaders you know into the different classifications shown in this short review about leadership.

Leadership is present in all organizational and social settings, and because organizational and social settings have sometimes diametrically different characteristics, leadership is perceived and conceptualized differently. It is important to understand that the perception of each person constitutes each one's reality. In addition, it is possible to say that you are not what you believe you are but what people believe you are. The same happens with leadership, people may believe that somebody is a leader while others see him or her as a tyrant. It is because of those different perceptions that we can explain why people define leadership in so many different ways. Some key leadership definitions include:

- Behaviors to direct... (Hemphill & Coons, 1957).
- Influence people using communication... (Tannenbaum, Weschler & Massarik, 1961).
- Initiation of structure ... (Stogdill, 1974).
- Use of communicational stimuli to affect cognitive-perceptual structures... (Yura, Ozimek & Walsh, 1976).
- Influence farther from routine work... (Katz & Kahn, 1978).
- The process to influence others' activities... (Rauch & Behling, 1984).
- The process to provide direction to collective efforts... (Jacobs & Jaques, 1990).
- Transformation of people toward high ethical and moral levels... (Bass and Avolio, 1994).

These definitions provide a good substrate to talk about leadership types, some of which include:

Autocratic, Democratic and Laissez Faire Leadership

Sargent and Miller (1971) described autocratic, democratic and laissez-faire leadership. Autocratic leaders give orders, reward, punish, and criticize followers. They tend to develop bad relations with their followers and tend to have a production-orientation without taking into account people's needs. Democratic leaders stimulate participation, suggest, provide support, promote self-discipline, and avoid unconstructive criticism. They tend to have good relations with their followers and tend to have a production and a group well-being-orientation. Laissez-faire leaders let the group lead itself, and tend to have neutral relationships with their followers.

Would you like to identify some leaders with the styles described above?

These leadership styles bring out different responses from their followers. Democratic leaders tend elicit higher satisfaction as well as compromise, group cohesion, creativity, and independence as compared to both autocratic and laissez-faire leaders. Autocratic leaders tend to maximize efficiency and productivity, when present, as compared to democratic leaders; however, autocratic leaders also elicit more hostility, aggression, and unexpressed annoyance as compared laissez-faire and autocratic leaders.

Autocratic leadership seems to be appropriate when tasks require structured processes, low compromise, initiative, or simplicity, when the leader is more knowledgeable than followers, and when time to complete the task is short.

Democratic leadership seems to be appropriate when tasks are complex, require different viewpoints, participation, creativity, and compromise.

Finally, laissez-faire leadership seems to be appropriate when people are highly competent and motivated, and when tasks require interdependence among people.

Tasks and Interpersonal Relationships

Leadership studies are also based on leaders' orientation toward work tasks and toward interpersonal relationships. Task-oriented leaders are characterized by their tendency to initiate structure to complete the tasks, and by their concern, mainly for production. Interpersonal relationship-oriented leaders are characterized by their consideration and concern for people.

Additionally, people-oriented leaders are characterized by their ability to disseminate information, ask for opinions, recognize others' viewpoints, have a flexible style of conversation, listen carefully, ask for ideas, focus on people's attitudes and needs, emphasize productivity through motivation, prefer oral communication, and keep an open-door policy.

On the other side, task-oriented leaders are characterized by their tendency to ignore others' viewpoints, use a rigid style of conversation, interrupt people, demand and request compliance, focus on facts and data related to the tasks, emphasize productivity through technical training, prefer writing communication, and keep a close door policy.

Researches of the University of Michigan, in the 1950s, by Rensis Likert define leadership on a continuum moving a production orientation to an employee orientation. Orientation toward production is characterized by a task- achievement focus, concentration on technical procedures, and tasks planning and organizing; orientation toward employees is characterized by a focus on employees' well-being, motivation, and development.

Simultaneously, Ohio State University's studies in the 1940s, based on the Leader Behavior Description Questionnaire (LBDQ), as Stodgill points out, define two dimensions of leadership: consideration and initiation of structure. Consideration includes aspects such as interpersonal orientation, expression of affection, feeling and ideas, and maintenance of a friendly work environment. Initiation of structure includes aspects such as focus on completion of tasks, initiating task activities, organizing and assigning tasks, and defining performance standards.

Again, we would like to make a pause at this point. Can you think of leaders who exhibit a people orientation, a production orientation, or both?

Theory X and Y

Douglas McGregor (1960) developed Theory X and Y, which describes managers' beliefs about people. Although his theory is more applicable to management situations, his premises may apply to leader-follower relationships. McGregor's dimension X establishes that many managers believe people are inherently averse to working. For this reason, managers obligate, control, direct, threat, and punish them. Managers assume responsibility for their employees' performance and achievement. McGregor's dimension Y establishes that many managers believe that people work adequately when provided with appropriate motivation. For this reason, managers challenge their followers, understand them, and motivate them. Managers assume that if they identify their subordinate's characteristics and provide subordinates with the right opportunities, tasks are accomplished effectively.

Managers with conception X tend to use coercive methods, control, and direction as the best ways to keep employees on the right track. They think that people like being supervised, controlled, and instructed about what and how to do things. They believe that organization needs, not employee needs, are of concern to a manager.

On the other hand, managers with a conception Y consider work a source of satisfaction in people and believe their employees consider work a natural activity to be engaged in. They believe that employees' dedication and pride are fundamental factors to increase productivity in an organization. A manager with a Y concept believes people want to feel responsible for their actions and want to participate in work tasks' design. Conception Y implies that people and organizational needs are equally important for managers.

Can you identify X leaders and Y leaders? Which conception do you identify with?

Blake y Mouton (1964) developed the Managerial Grid. They point out that leadership includes the components of employee motivation, socio-emotional relationships among people, and production and performance on tasks. These dimensions are similar to those described by University of Michigan and Ohio State University studies.

In 1961, Tannenbaum, Weschler y Massarik put forth - what we believe is the beginning of a holistic leadership view – that a leadership situation should include the leader, the followers, and the context characteristics. People become leaders because they chose to take the role and because the context and the followers ease their transformation. This, in few words, tells us that to be a leader, a person needs to choose to be one, the followers need to accept him or her as such and are willing to follow him or her, and the context has to be appropriate so that the leader can develop his or her leadership.

Situational Approaches

Contingent and Situational approaches identify environmental and contextual factors and followers as fundamental variables to describe leadership behaviors. We consider important to review three of these approaches. The first one, Fiedler's Contingency Theory, was developed in 1964 and is based on three variables: leader's power, task structure (established purposes, known task performance methods, known results, and pre-established verification mechanisms), and leader-follower relations. Fiedler establishes that leaders adopt two basic styles of leadership, concern for the tasks and concern for the followers. He asserts that good leader-followers relationships produce loyalty, affection, trust and respect toward the leader, while bad leader-followers' relationships produce low motivation and low compromise.

Situational approaches also include Path-Goal Theory. This theory proposes that motivation increases productivity when employees think that goal achievement is a path to obtain something valuable. In this approach, leaders can adopt directive, supportive, participative, and achievement-oriented styles.

Situational leadership development approach, developed by Hersey and Blanchard in the late 70s, states that managers and leaders exhibit two types of behaviors, similar to those studied by University of Michigan and Ohio State University and include concern for people and concern for production. Hersey and Blanchard also put forth the theory that these behaviors relate to people's work maturity. Work maturity involves motivation and competency. These factors can be combined to create high maturity (high motivation and competency), moderated maturity (high motivation and low competency, or low motivation and high competency), and low maturity (low motivation and low competency). The situational leadership development approach establishes that concern for people and concern for production when related to work maturity can be handled through four leadership styles: participative (share ideas and facilitate shared decision-making), persuasive or seller (explain and clarify decisions), delegating (provide freedom and responsibilities to followers), and telling (provides specific instruction and supervise performance).

Can you identify some leaders who use the styles described above? Which situational factors can you identify in your organization or in your work context? Using Hersey and Blanchard's definition of work maturity, what is the degree of work maturity of most members of your organization? What is your degree of work maturity?

Transactional and Transformational Approaches

In the last years, leadership studies conducted by James McGregor Burns (1978), Bennis y Nanus (985), and Bass and Avolio (1994), among others, put forth a new view of leadership, different from the approaches reviewed above, because they include some macro factors such as:

- Vision and mission design and communication
- The increase of compromise among collaborators
- The increase of effort from collaborators
- The increase of quality and productivity
- The empowerment of collaborators

These approaches, more comprehensive than the previous ones, include interrelations among people and organizations, a focus on people's development and transformation, organizational development and growth; these approaches consider the effects of leadership on internal and external organizations' contexts, and include moral and ethical issues as fundamental for leadership.

The purpose of this short review of leadership is to provide you a fundamental frame of reference for understanding leadership in organizations. We hope that you find the following section interesting and challenging and that it aids you in in thoughtfully considering leadership and leaders in your particular context.

The ladder of Transpersonal Leadership

Writing about leadership is a challenge, especially now that dramatic social changes are occurring, because leadership, as a social phenomenon, is changing. Leadership is one of the social processes most discussed but perhaps less agreed upon by people. People talk about leadership and leaders and people can, sometimes not accurately, identify and classify their leaders; however, many questions about leadership continue to emerge in everyday conversations, media coverage, and leadership development events. To us, people address many questions about leaders and leadership in leadership workshops and seminars. Questions that, we are sure, you have asked yourself. We want to start with these questions, so at the end of your reading, using as a basis the concepts presented in this book and your experience, you can answer them. Some of the questions more frequently asked in our leadership development workshops and seminars are as follows:

- Does leadership emerge spontaneously or is it developed?
- Are leaders born or are developed?
- What are the strategies leaders must implement to bring about organizational change?
- How do we know when leadership has been successful?
- What are the characteristics of effective leaders?
- Can autocratic leaders be successful in their organizations?
- How do we deal with "negative" leaders?
- How do leaders develop leadership in a globalized era?
- How can leaders influence workers' attitudes?
- How can leaders motivate personnel in adverse situations?
- How do leaders channel leadership toward general well-being?
- What tools can leaders use to create a pleasant atmosphere, solve problems and promote effective work?
- How do leaders achieve empathy with their team members?
- How should leaders respond to those who do not comply with their responsibilities?

Writing about The Ladder of Transpersonal Leadership made us revisit these questions, especially when people asked us to compare two leaders, for example, "Hitler and Jesus Christ."

Then and today, we believe that leadership is a social process that seeks people's lasting well-being. Those who set Hitler and Jesus Christ as leaders have an unclear, nonsocial conception about leadership. We believe that people have in their minds philosophical and practical contradictions about leadership. We believe that perhaps one of the reasons for which people consider some barbarous or destructive individuals in extremist groups as leaders is because they do not know, or do not understand the pro-social dimension of leadership or have a very narrow conception of leadership. Ask yourself, what is going on in our society when, in the name of religion or of membership in an ethnic group, some people are destroying lives? Could it be that some people see in these so-called leaders what they always have wanted to be and never have been? Could it be that some people are projecting themselves on these so-called leaders? If this is the case, we need to review the messages our leaders are sending to society. We need to vet what messages opinion agents, politicians, judges, teachers, journalists, organization CEOs, and anybody with the power to frame people's attitudes are sending to the common citizen.

Writing about Transpersonal leadership was, initially, the result of the free flow of reflections, without directionality, about what people need to know about leadership as evidenced by the questions shown. However, we realized that experiencing non-directionality was beneficial in that it kept us reflecting about our experience, others' experiences, and the theories and approaches about leadership. We understood that people have a limited, old-fashioned notion about leadership no longer appropriate for our globalized planet. Transpersonal leadership and the Ladder of Leadership was the result of a deductive-inductive process that helps us to confront surprising, and sometimes inconsistent, events of leaders' work and of leadership processes; we experienced personally some of these events, and sometimes we have lived them through others' experiences. This deductive-inductive process made us aware that not everyone who influences is a leader, and made us seek answers in relation to what real leadership is and who "real" leaders are. We hope that when you finish this reading, your ideas about leadership and Transpersonal leadership are as clear as ours are. We expect that you agree with us. However, if you do not, we will at least be content that you have thought about it.

Besides the theoretical framework, we base our views of leaders and Transpersonal leadership on the experiences obtained through workshops, seminars, and courses taught to over seven hundred managers and leaders of social, health, manufacturing, and education service organizations, among others. The *Ladder of Transpersonal Leadership* explains the different existing conceptions about leaders and leadership, especially those in which people who have taken socially undesirable actions - in different social contexts and in light of historical developments - are categorized as leaders. This is why some people consider characters like Hitler, Napoleon Bonaparte, Fidel Castro, and others who you may have in mind now, as leaders while others consider them as tyrants or barbarians. A fundamental problem arises when you put all these people in the same category – when you classify all of them as leaders – you are seeing leadership social dimension in an incorrect and simplified way.

We believe, therefore, that to be a leader it is not enough to move people in a certain direction. We believe that this notion diminishes our role in leadership by leaving the responsibility to direct our actions only in the hands of the leader, our communities, the society, or the country where we live. If we accept this view of leadership, we surrender our role within the social dynamics and became the followers of "orders" given by a person who may take us, because of his or her ignorance or convenience, in any direction, sometimes toward an abyss in which we may even be unable to survive. If we accept this conception of leaders and leadership, we are renouncing our right to establish and to assert our points of view, and we delegate our right to decide. We stop practicing a critical and developmental followership.

The definition of leadership as the ability to influence others makes equal leaders who have acted to reach organizational objectives, thinking on the society and in the well-being and development of people and leaders who have acted moved by personal interests – egomaniacs - without regard to the well-being and development of their fellows in the same category. Additionally, this conception of leadership perpetuates the idea of higher and lower, leaders and followers, knowledgeable and ignorant; it perpetuates the idea that the leader knows what to do and most people should accept uncritically what he or she tells them. Of course, within those extremes, there are different types of leaders that allow followers' participation in decision-making. At one end, there are "leaders" who do not accept suggestions from his followers, thus becoming dictators in their contexts (family, community, or country). Tyrants do not accept others' points of view and may even threaten the physical integrity of those who do not act as they wish. Leadership, seen only as the process to influence people, also implies that the purpose is subordinate to the leader and that followers should rotate around their leader's desires. At the other end, there are leaders who believe that people, and their personal and social development, are the basis of the leadership process. Leaders who believe that social participation and shared decision-making are foundation stones of an effective social dynamic. They see others as collaborators, not as followers, who are part of a process of change in which all are partners and active participants.

A scheme of transpersonal leadership requires that leader and collaborators operate on the purpose that organization and society members have defined as desirable. In this sense, Transpersonal leadership is directly aligned with democracy, as a political and social form of relationship, in which the well-being and the participation of all those who make up society are fundamental. We are confident that under this perspective, some so-called leaders should not be in the leadership category. It is necessary to define and determine what those people are. It is necessary to define leadership in a broader and more complex context within a period that goes beyond a short time frame. It is necessary to include in the definition the processes, social results, and their impacts on people, followers, leaders, and on the environment, instead of defining leadership as a process of influence.

Transpersonal leadership is the result of the analysis of different leadership theories and approaches, of the review of the performance of some leaders, and of the experiences in multiple workshops about leadership development, which included different types of participants, coming from public and private, profit and non-profit organizations. Transpersonal leadership is a theoretical approach that helps us set leaders at different stages of leadership development. The transpersonal leadership ladder helps us to assess leaders according to their behaviors and to place them in the stage of development they belong. The transpersonal leadership ladder includes five steps that describe the social development of the leader. These are: (1) influencing people; (2) influencing by appealing to ethical and moral principles; (3) promoting and facilitating the development of people and the organization; (4) acting with a socio-centric orientation; and (5) acting with a global and ecological orientation.

The ladder of transpersonal leadership

Practicing a global and ecological orientation

Developing and practicing a socio-centric attitude

Promoting and facilitating people's and organization's development

Influencing using ethical and moral principles socially acceptable

Influencing people

"Leadership is not magnetic personality that can just as well be a glib tongue. It is not 'making friends and influencing people', that is flattery. Leadership is lifting a person's vision to higher sights, the raising of a person's performance to a higher standard, the building of a personality beyond its normal limitations."

Peter F. Drucker

1. Influencing people

Influencing people, the first step of the transpersonal leadership ladder has to do with the leader's ability to move others in a certain direction. It has to do with the ability to make people do what the leader thinks should be done. There are no value judgments associated with the means or mechanisms the leader uses to achieve the objectives. In addition, there are no value judgments regarding the reasons the leader has to move people; reasons may be associated with an egocentric or socio-centered point of view, with altruistic purposes or not, with pro-social processes or with personal desires. In synthesis, the first step establishes that leaders are individuals who influence others. It is this step where we can place, without distinction, people like Adolfo Hitler, Fidel Castro, Winston Churchill, Napoleon Bonaparte, Simon Bolívar, Juan Pablo II, and the Pope Francisco, among others. All of them have something in common. They influenced others. Think about leaders that have reached this step. Are there many of them?

Influencing others is directly related to what in the 60's and 70's was regarded as leadership, when definitions to categorize one person as a positive or a negative leader, depending on the results of his or her influence, were developed. In this step, the fiercest discussions about who leaders are and what leadership took place. People who define leadership as the ability to influence say that Hitler, though he caused great evils to the world and his followers, was a leader, say that Christ, Fidel Castro, and Mother Teresa are equally leaders, and say that leadership is relative and depends on the society where the leader develops as such.

We allow ourselves a deviation from the fundamental topic of this chapter to introduce an idea about the nature of the influence in leadership. Leadership relates to the well-being of the follower, to the respect for others, and to the recognition of people's diversity - race, thoughts, beliefs, and points of view. This view sets leadership within a much broader context than the one that establishes that one person is a leader because he or she influenced on his or her family, community, and country, even when he or she caused harm to those close and/or far. In other words, the consideration of a broad global context sets leadership in a much more complex situation that makes it difficult to categorize, without distinction, all the above-named people as leaders. A broader context can be the neighboring community or another country, if we speak in terms of organizations, it may be other organizations, the community where the organization operates, or the country where the organization is.

Leadership merely defined as influencing others and pro- and anti-social behaviors not differentiated as appropriate or inappropriate leadership behaviors over simplify the leadership definition and the social role of the leader. This definition, frequently used in many contexts, especially mass media, does not explain the true essence of leadership, which is to influence to favor the well-being of the people.

At this point, we allow ourselves to ask some questions you should keep in mind to continue climbing the ladder. Who of those that you consider leaders are in this step? How do you categorize leaders who have influenced people to undertake a position against other people? Is their ability to influence condition enough to call them a leader? How have leaders influenced you?

The next paragraphs will help you to answer some of these questions. Influence, from the collective point of view, is a key element of leadership. However, it is uncommon to know how leaders influence their followers.

Types of influence

Influence has to do with moving people in a direction. A person influences others when they believe or do what the person wants. We are sure you have heard people saying, "Hitler influenced a large a number of German nationals because they did what he wanted." Certainly, they did it, and they exterminated millions of people during the war.

Influence has to do with "movement", the action that a person, conscious or unconsciously, undertakes when asked to do something. There are different ways to influence, using different tactics. We describe some tactics based on the works made by Yukl in 1994, published in his book *Leadership in Organizations*. He sets up that tactics of influence are actions that leaders, in a conscious or unconscious way, take to move people in the desired direction. The tactics of influence, we discuss below, include rational persuasion, emotional persuasion, consultation, ingratiation, personal interest, transaction, coalition, legitimacy, and pressure.

Rational persuasion

Rational persuasion has to do with the use of rational "objective" arguments and evidence by the leader to make people do things or move in a certain direction. The leader who selects this tactic uses factors and elements that followers assess as logical, valuable or desirable, and useful from a social and contextual definition. The leader uses rational arguments shared by the majority, and he or she leaves out "human" and emotional opinions. Rational persuasion is, in Western society, a fundamental way to make decisions and a cornerstone in defining people's actions. Rational persuasion is one of the most widely used forms to influence people, and although it is associated with objectivity, but as you know, "objectivity is in the eye of the beholder".

Rational persuasion relates to the Aristotelian thought, which suggests that what is logical is suitable, and consequently provides a "desirable" outcome. However, we believe that this kind of logic, based on few elements, ignores the existence and complexity of a network of inter-relationships that operate in those social events where leadership occurs.

Considering logic only to define the key elements to take into account to decide about leader-followers interactions leaves out the interrelationships and recurrent unapparent, non-concrete and subjective factors – the personal feelings involved in the process of leadership. Influencing people using rational persuasion works successfully only when the leader convinces people that the rational components of a situation are the fundamentals, when the followers avoid including or ignoring the emotional components, or when they do not know how emotions affect their contexts.

Some military "leaders" using rational persuasion argue that the loss of a number of people in a battle is acceptable because the costs and benefits justify it. This position, which seems logical and rational, leaves out the value and the emotions associated with the loss of human lives. Can you think of something more illogical and irrational than justifying the loss of even one human being? Ask yourself, have you known leaders who made decisions based on a "logic" that led to unintended results? When we used logic-rational arguments, are we confident that we have included all the factors involved in the situation? Is rational persuasion "broad enough" to include all different logical views of the stakeholders? Is the leader rationally aligned with his or her followers, or of those affected by the decision?

If you do not have all the answers, do not worry. We will address these questions ahead, in the section about ethics of leadership. There, we will review the relationship between rational decision-making and the ethical implications of those decisions.

Idealistic persuasion

Idealistic persuasion, also called emotional persuasion by some authors, is a tactic of influence whereby the leader uses followers' values, ideals, and aspirations to convince them of the need to take some course of action. Idealistic persuasion moves arguments to a field where cultural, social, emotional or personal reasons are valuable and desirable to ponder to make decisions. When the leader uses this form of persuasion, he or she appeals to collaborators' guiding principles and values to convince them to follow his or her idea or proposal.

The use of idealistic persuasion moves the arguments from apparent objectivity towards what people believe produces well-being-- even though, in many cases, they do not have specific and factual evidence on how these proclaimed ideas or values will benefit them. For example, leaders use elements of nationalism, love for country, and preservation of group superiority to amalgamate people against a supposed common enemy. At this point, can you think about leaders who have used "nationalism " as a "flag" to achieve their ends?

Many "charismatic" leaders who want to remain in power and ensure that followers act in accordance with their desires, which may be contrary to the well-being of all, wrongly use idealistic persuasion. On the other hand, idealist persuasion, in its purest and most desirable form, has to do with the use of ideals, based on socially shared ethical and moral principles, to persuade a leader's collaborators of a particular course of action. Leaders use the idealistic persuasion by appealing to the culture of their followers, which includes philosophy, beliefs, values, principles, and ways of acting shared by their social groups. The leader who practices this form of persuasion, to move his followers, identifies and uses those cultural elements to achieve his or her ends.

Leadership literature is full of stories in which leaders have used idealistic persuasion as a means or a mechanism, alone or combined with other forms of persuasion, to make people do what they want. The case of Hitler is an example. He appealed to the reconstruction of the country, argued for a better standard of living for Germans, and lured people with the idea of a superior Aryan race. He "sold" the ideas of "nationalism" and "white supremacy" to Germans regardless of the consequences on other people. He took advantage of the German population's extreme needs caused by a combination of previously unfulfilled promises and of political and social problems. Followers were not prepared psychologically and sociologically to deal with these ideas. They had diminished self-concepts and empathy, were suffering dramatic shortages of resources, and were looking for a messiah to save them. Germans were unable to see the manipulation and to take into account the inherent value of others and the impact of their decisions on those who thought differently. The consequences of the use of idealistic persuasion, in this example, were fatal to Germans, and to the world.

The idealistic persuasion, as a fundamental form of persuasion, is what characterizes leaders who have emerged as tyrants after some time. It is interesting to realize how, in the least developed countries, and now in some developed countries, where economic, social, and psychological issues are prevalent, "charismatic" leaders arise. They often emerge preaching pseudo-values and nationalist ideas as justification for unethical actions. Holy wars, attacking residents of a country and destruction of ethnic groups are justified using idealistic assumptions. In these cases, the leaders have used idealistic persuasion as a tactic to move people to pursue actions that, we know now, have produced anti-social results. In the first, second, third, or whatever "world", the crisis caused by the lack of attention to the basic needs of the population, their lack of education, and low self-esteem has created fertile land to grow pseudo-leaders who use wrongly idealistic persuasion.

This description applies to countries such as Cuba, Venezuela, Somalia, but can increasingly apply to countries such as Germany, Italy, France, and even the United States. In these nations, leaders' claims may differ in their content – it may be nationalism, immigration, refuges, supremacy, and grandiosity - but all o have something in common. Leaders want to convince and to push people to behave in some ways by using emotions and subjective information that, in most of the cases, obscure the basis considerations of respect for other people, and for cultural diversity. These leaders simply are deceiving their people.

Consultation

Consultation is based on the assumption that participation makes people move, in a voluntary way, towards the accomplishment of the activities proposed by the leader. Consultation is a tactic that involves stakeholders in making decisions and taking actions to achieve the goals the leader wants to achieve. Stakeholders intervene in the design of processes and procedures to do so. Leaders who use consultation show respect for their collaborators and recognize that diverse opinions help make decisions more achievable and effective as compared to those the leader makes alone.

The leader who consults to influence contributes to the personal and social development of his or her collaborators, and as added value, demonstrates the importance of participation, and therefore of democracy, in the leadership process. In addition, in complex situations, where there is a multiplicity of factors involved as we see today, consultation constitutes a resource to effectively reach the goals, implement the strategies and carry out the change processes effectively.

Leaders, depending on their democratic conception, can use different forms of consultation. The leader can adopt a distributed, direct, and comprehensive consultation that includes all parties involved in the action, which is the most democratic and participative form of leadership. On the other hand, the leader can adopt the practice of consulting with collaborators' representatives, which constitutes a representative-democratic position. In either case, the leader achieves participation and commitment, although to different degrees. We believe that commitment is higher using the first approach. However, sometimes, limited consultation to a small group is advisable because of time, cost, and limited stakeholder's knowledge of the issue. Consultation requires more time to arrive at conclusions and to implement decisions, but, on the other hand, leaders who use consultation increase their ability to influence.

Consultation, as we have previously explained, is widely used by leaders who want to encourage the development of their collaborators. Consultation involves a challenge of ideas, which brings conclusions that are more comprehensive and guarantees the participants' identification with the decisions. Situations where consultation is limited to a group close to the leader have the potential of rejection due to low participation of collaborators. If the leader must use a restricted consultation tactic, he or she must clearly explain when, how, and especially why this type of consultation is made in order to retain the ability to influence properly people in the future. The leader who uses consultation should embrace and discuss collaborators' suggestions and ideas and should implement them. If a leader consults collaborators but their ideas are not used, they may become frustrated and alienated. Think about, how you feel when you propose an idea and it is not taken into account. How do you feel? Do you feel alienated and frustrated?

Ingratiation

Ingratiation is a tactic of influence based on the use of praise, flattery, "friendly" behavior and unconditional support to make people do what the leader wants. The leader who uses this tactic often exploits the followers' desire for admiration and recognition. The use of this tactic moves leadership from a complex socio-relational process, whose purpose is to make people aware that their actions should be socially oriented, to a personal relationship, in which the complacency of the followers' desires is the strategy the leader uses to ensure they act in the way he or she wants. In other words, Ingratiation implies that the leader uses individuals' desires and not people's social principles to influence them.

The use of the ingratiation to influence can drive followers to bitterness and frustration when the leader flattery and praises positive features that the collaborators recognize they do not have. When followers recognize that they were convinced to take action with arguments that have nothing to do with their beliefs and values, and when they realize that the promised support will never materialize.

Followers with a strong need for recognition, who are motivationally immature, externally motivated, and who need incentives and resources that they cannot get by themselves are easily persuaded through ingratiation. On the other hand, mature collaborators, those who want to contribute and know how to act in a socially orientated way, reject ingratiation. They are internally motivated - they know what they need and how to get it, know their peers' capabilities, and are aware of their own capabilities and developmental needs; for this reason, using ingratiation to influence mature people is ineffective. Mature collaborators see the leader who uses ingratiation as adulating, insincere, and hypocritical.

Can you think of leaders who have used ingratiation as a tactic to influence you? In the end, what did you think about them?

Personal connection

Personal connection, as a tactic to influence, appeals to followers' feelings of loyalty and friendship toward the leader. Leaders who know that their followers are loyal and friendly use these feelings as "arguments" to move them in the desired direction. This tactic appeals to elements that do not originate in the ability to persuade others because of the desirability of a leader's purposes but in links or connections established with people. This tactic of influence could make followers take action against a person, an organization, and a group just because the leader is their "friend." Leaders who have shared life experiences and work situations with some people rely on feelings of friendship previously developed, and they use these feelings to move people to do what they want.

The leader who uses personal connection appeals to followers' gratitude to induce them to take an action. In many cases, the leader uses his or her friendship with one follower or with a small group of followers - for example, a friendship developed in the past in a different context - to push everybody to do what he or she wants to be done, regardless of whether it is socially acceptable or convenient for all.

Transaction

The transaction, as a tactic to influence, involves the exchange of favors or promises and the sharing of benefits between the leader and the collaborators, so they do what he or she expects. In the transaction, the leader identifies followers' wants, drives, and needs and offers them to satisfy these desires in order to gain their commitment to his or her cause.

In a transaction, the leader provides followers with the resources or favors their needs – things such as promotions, money rewards, the hiring of a family member or a friend and in the worst cases, the payment of money and the granting of resources - to receive in exchange their support. The leader can combine transaction and ingratiation, whereupon he or she influences followers by providing them with the specific desired goods and recognition - tangible and psychological rewards.

A transaction could move the leader and followers outside of the value of social issues and of the generation of socially desirable goals into corruption. Followers are corrupted when the leader gives them something they have not "won" and do not deserve. In these cases, transactions are unethical. The leader who uses these incentives to influence followers perverts socially desirable and accepted schemes of behavior, first, by making transactions with resources that do not belong to him or her, second, by creating an attitude of little commitment toward social achievements and work completion, and third, by only trading concrete incentives and rewards.

History includes many "leaders" who have used transactions in negative ways. Some leaders have done ignominious and miserable transactions by taking resources from the followers and then providing some type of "wellness" to them. The leader deprives followers of resources and then the leader gives them something to create the illusion that he or she is a savior. In exchange, the leader receives followers' unconditional support. Many leaders take advantage of underprivileged people, who have few possessions and knowledge, and ask them for support in exchange for political positions, which in most cases includes material and social privileges. Sometimes followers who get these privileges focus on getting what they have never had by using methods that go against the social structure, and by taking resources that belong to other people. The leader and the followers who participate in these transactions damage the society and corrupt people. Do you know any leaders with these characteristics? Do you know leaders who use this tactic?

Coalition

The Coalition, as a tactic to influence, seeks to back the idea or activity that the leader wants to achieve through the formation of alliances with a group of followers or with other leaders. A coalition supported by different social segments who want to solve a common problem produces a synergetic solution feasible to implement. On the other hand, the leader who establishes coalitions with small groups, not representative of the whole society, degrades leadership and may become the chief of a gang, or of a clan, instead of a leader. Usually, this type of coalition produces undesirable results for the majority. It is an aberration of the leadership process. It makes followers lose confidence in their leaders, develop apathy, and finally, increase the desire not to participate organizational and social issues.

The coalition implies that the leader, unable to convince his followers because the proposal is not desired or because he or she do not have enough support, seeks to influence people by asking for the help of those who are perceived as opinion leaders and social drivers. The leader who negotiates something that is desirable for the followers is using coalition and transaction tactics. We believe that the coalition done without thinking in socially desirable principles may generate rejection from those who did not intervene in it. Typical cases of coalitions are the political alliances made in the parliament of a country in order to vote for a certain rule or law or to select a person for government positions when the parties cannot achieve a solution by consensus. Can you think how many times such coalitions have resulted in problems and heinous situations? Can you think of coalitions made between countries that later become enemies?

A decision made using coalition and transaction usually creates problems to be implemented, and it usually gets against the social groups and the subjects who made the decision, especially, when the results of the decision are not desired anymore, or when the decision, in the long run, is ineffective. In many countries, the selection of public authorities follows this pattern. Many political groups or "social organizations" have developed coalitions to select people who later prove to be inefficient and act against the groups who intervened in the coalition. This situation is common in many organizations when somebody is appointed to a position without pondering his or her performance, efficiency, legal, social, and ethical principles but rather focus on the exchange of privileges or of power. Think in situations in your context, where transaction and coalition are used to select organizational, community, and regional "leaders", or to select government officials. What consequences have such selections brought out?

Legitimation

The leaders who invoke their authority or "right" to lead are using legitimation as a tactic to influence. People accept a leader's influence because it is consistent with the policies, rules, practices, traditions, and laws. Legitimation implies that the leader uses the authority given by the position - granted by a legal or social mandate - to move his or her followers in one direction. The main problem of legitimation is that relies on an external element - a rule or a norm - that does not "belong" to the leader. In many cases, followers may decide not to accept the "legitimacy" of their leader as it has happened during rebellions. In many rebellions, the leader needs to use pressure or coercion to recuperate his or her capability to influence because followers do not want to accept the "leader's authority" anymore. In these cases, the leader is delegitimized. It is important to remember that a leader's legitimacy does not come from actions and behaviors but from a social contract or from cultural practices, which may not be inherent to the leader. Additionally, when using legitimation, the leader's ability to influence followers does not derive from his or her personal competence nor from the admiration that followers feel toward the leader.

Effective legitimation is present when followers share and accept their leader's legitimacy and when the leader is able to maintain it over time. The leader cannot use this tactic to influence when he or she is de-legitimized. Leader de-legitimation occurs, in many organizations, social groups, and countries when a person selected for a position by election, because of legal rights, or because of organizational rules after having broad followers' support, loses its capacity to influence. This happens when a leader is unable to handle situations appropriately or because is unable to fulfill his or her initial offerings.

Legitimation works as far as it results in benefits to the followers. In fact, leaders using this tactic and achieving the desired results increase their legitimacy, the followers trust them, and the leader confidently and effectively can use his or her legitimate power in future situations. The leader who uses legitimation and does not produce socially desirable results produces disenchantment, opposition and resistance to take the action he or she suggests.

Elected and appointed leaders must move from normative or legal legitimacy to performance legitimacy. Performance legitimacy fortifies leader-influence in critical moments when an emergency or necessity requires they make decisions without consulting followers. Leaders legitimized by their performance do not need to use the authority provided by laws or existing social norms.

Social dynamics, in today's turbulent environments, require that the leader, to remain as such, develop performance legitimacy and perform in such a way that the majority of the followers benefit personally and socially. Can you identify elected or selected leaders who have become legitimized for their positive performance and who have become de-legitimized because of their bad performances?

Pressure

Pressure, as a tactic to influence, uses threats, frequent checking or persistent reminders, to move people in the desired direction. Pressure places the responsibility for action on the leader, who must exercise it for the followers to act. The leader pushes followers who do not want to undertake actions by their own conviction. Leaders who continuously use pressure may have lost their ability to influence followers through other tactics. When this happens, the pressure may produce followers' resistance. The resistance may emerge as disobedience at the time the leader cannot put more pressure on the followers. Pressure operates properly while the leader has the ability to provide punishments deemed undesirable by followers. Pressure also generates resistance and disobedience when followers acquire resources that ease the undesirability of the pressure, learn to avoid the punishment by other means, or become aware the leader wants them to do something against their integrity.

Pressure is usually linked to other forms of influence such as transaction, ingratiation, and personal connection. The leader can use these using concrete or psychological elements, and followers may develop feelings of submissiveness and of being abused, which might produce a growing feeling of despondency or an increased desire to rebel. Continuous use of pressure, progressively, reduces a leader's ability to lead. He or she loses his or her authority and power, and people may rather prefer the punishment and the reprobation than accepting their leader's requests.

Leaders influence people in different ways, using different tactics. They often rely on several tactics at the same time. We have shown some of the tactics leaders can use, so you reflect about them and search examples in your context, in your family, in your organization, in your workplace, and in your social environment. It is valuable to let you find how you have experienced these tactics. It is important that you categorize those leaders who you have been with according to the tactics they have used. We believe that your ideas and experiences with those leaders have certainly more learning value than the experiences we can give you. Please, think about them.

After the summary, we will describe the second step to ascend to transpersonal leadership. In this step, we include the types of power leaders may use, and some examples you can take as points of reference to interpret leaders' behaviors within the context of transpersonal leadership.

Summary

The first step, influencing people, has to do with leader's ability to move people in a certain direction. People using this definition say that Hitler, Jesus Christ, Fidel Castro and Mother Teresa of Calcutta are leaders.

Influencing people as the main element in defining leadership is an oversimplification of the leadership process and of its social dimension. Do you think that the ability to influence is a sufficient condition to categorize a person as a leader?

Some tactics of influence that leaders use include rational persuasion (the use of rational arguments and verifiable evidence), idealistic persuasion (the use of values, ideals, and aspirations), consultation (asking followers for their participation in the design of the actions to be followed), ingratiation (the use of praise, flattery and friendly behavior to convince people), personal connection (appealing to loyalty and friendship), transaction (the exchange of desired resources), coalition (the formation of partnerships), legitimation (the use of normative authority), and pressure (the use of persistent reminders and frequent control).

Tactics of influence

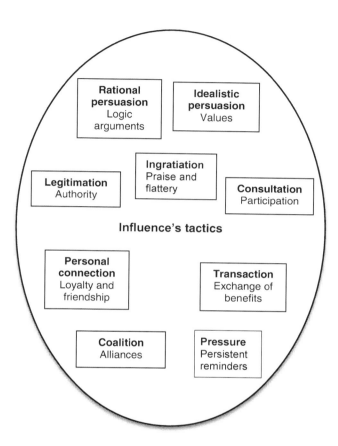

"If the blind lead the blind, both shall fall in the ditch."

Jesus Christ

2. Influencing by appealing to moral and ethical, socially accepted principles that produce well-being in collaborators

The second step asserts, as does the previous, that leaders influence people. However, this step deals with a quality dimension-- exerting influence "appropriately." To do so, it is necessary to appeal to moral and ethical, socially accepted, principles that produce well-being in collaborators. This step establishes that leaders should not use rewards, punishments, or penalties but requires a people-centered orientation. The leader who expresses, unquestionably, high consideration for the value of contributors' opinions and viewpoints of others takes a people-centered orientation where. The types of power used by the leader, and the ethical and moral consequences associated with the use of such power, are critical to understanding this step. In this step, we review the types of power used by the leader to influence his or her followers.

Types of power

The bases of power that we describe rely on the tenets of French and Raven described in their work *The Bases of Social Power*, in 1959. These bases include expert power, reference power, reward and coercive power, and legitimate power. Additionally, we include the power based on possession of information. We analyze these power bases in relation to followers' participation.

Power is the potential ability to influence. In fact, influence is the result of turning this potentiality into action. In common terms, a leader can have one or several types of power yet not influence people because they do not do what the leader asks. In the context of leadership, it is not enough to possess the power but it is necessary that the people, on whom power is exercised, accept it, consciously or unconsciously, and move in the direction the leader wants. It is so when a leader influences followers. In the following paragraphs, we describe the types of power or "he bases of power" as called by French and Raven.

Legitimate power

Legitimate power is given by the position the leader occupies either because it is socially accepted, social norms defined it so or because an organization establishes it; it is associated with the position of the leader in the context where it operates, be this context familial, social, political or organizational.

Leaders who are selected or elected to high posts, within a hierarchical, legal, or socially accepted scheme, possess the power that gives them the position. In other words, the position gives them the potential to influence, regardless of they do it or not. Legitimate power relates to legitimation as a form of influence. For example, the head of the family, by social reasons, has the authority to influence his children. However, we know that in many cases, some parents fail to do so, because when it comes to exercise legitimate power, children do not accept the authority given by "hierarchical reasons" and do not agree on their parent's requests. Followers who do not accept the "hierarchical model" disobey and challenge leader's authority.

In the military, we find good examples to show how a commander's legitimate power may turn illegitimate because of his or her actions. The commander of a group has for normative, legal, and regulatory reasons control and authority over his or her command. Subordinates accept this authority over them because they shared those norms, laws, and regulations. The commander who moves out of that regulatory or constitutional frame of reference - for example, leads a coup d'état, or gives an order against legal, social, moral, and ethical viewpoints may be challenged by his subordinates and considered illegitimate. If they do not do so, they will become as illegitimate as their commander. The regime and the leadership that emerges after such action have no legitimate power.

A leader can have all power bases and have absolute power, but in the end, his or her power will be illegitimate if it goes against the norms and the law. Absolute power corrupts, and even the most psychologically well-balanced human beings have succumbed to the seduction of absolute power. The leader can use legitimate power appropriately and avoid capitulating to that seduction by showing respect for others, self-control, and fairness, and by being aware that the legitimate power he or she has is due to the position he or she occupies-- it belongs to the position, is not part of his or her "being."

Reward and coercive power

Reward and coercive power have to do with the leader's ability to provide followers with something that they deem desirable or undesirable. Reward and coercive power are two sides of the same coin. In other words, the leader who can give something that followers want, need, or use, whether these are material, social and psychological recompenses, has reward power. On the other hand, the leader who can provide punishment to followers - remove elements that serve to meet their needs and penalize them physically or psychologically - has coercive power. The leader has the power to reward and to coerce as long as he or she has access to rewards or punishments deemed desirable or undesirable by collaborators. It is an objectionable form of power because it gives the leader the ability to influence his followers by providing or depriving them of something they need and not because he or she gained their respect and support.

Coercive and reward power are exercised by the leader who has the ability to manage what is deemed undesirable or desirable by followers. However, the indiscriminate use of punishment and rewards can lead people to them as less repulsive or valuable than the leader sees them, and reward and coercive powers may lose their potential to influence. People become unaffected by rewards and penalizations when they are used repeatedly. A classic example is a child who has received physical punishment continuously; in some moment, he or she rebels against and says, "did you finish?" or "do you have something else?"

Rewards and punishment, as forms of exercising power, relate closely to the transaction, which is a form of influence. Rewards and punishments work while followers have not found substitutes to the rewards or punishments. For example, a substitute to a reward may be being part of a social movement or being part of a process to achieve political freedom. In these cases, a higher-level reward substitutes a previous low-order reward; in the case of punishment, some people assimilate punishment to a point where it does not reach enough physical or psychological aversion, and it simply does not bring the results wanted by the punisher.

Expert power

Expert power is based on the experience and the knowledge that a leader has in a work area, context, or situation. The person who possesses it has the ability to influence because he or she knows how to do things. Supporters recognize the leader's knowledge, skills, and abilities, and, therefore, follow and accept the leader's role. Expert power does not necessarily relate to a leader's formal education but rather has to do with his or her knowledge in those areas that he or she is leading. Expert power constitutes one of the fundamental ways to lead properly because, even if the leader is not a specialist in a specific area, he or she is able to understand the factors involved in the situations he or she confronts.

Expert power makes collaborators feel confident of leaders' actions and decisions. Collaborators follow the leader they believe is capable, knowledgeable, and skillful to handle situations. The leader is competent, and this competency gives the leader power. Essentially, collaborators follow the can work effectively with them. Expert power increases its potential to produce influence when it is linked to rational persuasion. However, the leader must use expert power carefully, especially with supporters who possess a lower level of competency and knowledge. When a leader's knowledge is greater than that of his or her supporters, he or she must recognize supporters' contributions and participation and uses his or her knowledge in a way that collaborators do not feel diminished. On the other hand, the expert power used with supporters who possess a very low knowledge may make them feel that a leader is a special person, followers may project their needs on the leader, and do what the leader suggests without questioning because they do not know the leader may be doing something inappropriate. Therefore, the development - the acquisition of knowledge, skills, and abilities - of followers is essential to creating a transpersonal leadership, in which supporters are able and feel free to provide feedback that allows adjustments when the leadership process is not producing the desired results.

Reference power

Reference power relates to the admiration, appreciation, and esteem followers feel for their leader. This power is not clearly associated with a specific and an easily discernible feature. It has to do with "that" feeling some followers experience when they express "We do not know why but when the leader talks, we want to follow him." Reference power relates to what some authors call charismatic leadership. The causes of a leader's referent power are hard to determine, as it is a kind of power difficult to explain. Because of this, some people simply, without knowing why, follow the leader. Reference power has nothing to do with magic or a *Je ne sais pas quoi* that leaders possess but it may include subjective elements that followers, unconsciously, perceive as desirable. It may relate to a leader's warmness when establishing relationships with the people, to an "unexplained" authority that he or she "radiates," to his or her friendly and open communication style, and to the respect that he or she shows when relating to people.

Reference power is linked to a series of "soft competencies" or "invisible competencies" such as active listening, warm communication, comprehensiveness, attentiveness, empathy, and sympathy, among others, which have not been studied thoroughly so far. Leadership scholars are studying these competencies more profoundly, through research and in leadership training and development events.

People who have skills to interact with others have reference power. This type of power seems to be primarily based on people's admiration and identification with the leader. Leaders with high reference power show concern for their supporters and, when necessary, advocate for them, show desire to integrate people, take action beyond expected when needed, and show understanding of others' viewpoints. Collaborators look actively for their leader's approval when he or she has reference power.

Power for possession of information

The power by possession of information relates to the leader's access to sources of information that may facilitate effective decision-making and to the leader's ability to provide data and information that allows followers to do their work effectively. Collaborators believe that leaders who have access to information are able to guide them properly.

Power by possession of information relates also to the leader's ability to keep abreast with what is happening... Informed leaders make decisions that are more effective, and followers perceive them as people who have the authority to guide them in the right direction. Possession of information power gives the leader the ability to influence by using data and information that are desirable and important for supporters, and, therefore, relates to rational persuasion.

Power, defined as the potential to influence, determines the ability of leaders to move their followers in a certain direction. Some of the bases of power described in the previous paragraphs, such as expert, referent, and for possession of information, are most appropriate to ascend the transpersonal leadership ladder in a socially acceptable manner, while reward and coercive, and legitimate power, move the leader outside their pro-social orientation. Pro-social leaders must be able to use forms of power suitable to and socially accepted by followers. The use of socially based powers, which do not degrade followers, allows the leader to continue rising on the transpersonal leadership ladder. It is what will enable him or her to continue to the next step: promoting and facilitating followers' development.

What types of power some leaders you know have used? What are the most appropriate forms of power a leader needs to climb on to the second step? Remember when you were in a leadership position. Which type of power did you use more frequently?

Summary

The second step, influencing by appealing to ethical and moral principles, which are socially accepted-- as opposed to the rewards of low order and coercion-- has to do with the power bases.

Power is the potential ability to influence. Influence is, indeed, the result of the exercise of power. The Leaders influence when they use power, but the ability to influence is not sufficient to consider a person as a leader; it is necessary to influence using ethical and moral elements that are socially accepted.

In this step, we consider the power of the leader in several forms. They included: legitimate power (conferred by the position of the leader in accordance with established standards), reward and coercive power (ability of the leader to provide something desirable or undesirable), expert power (based on leader's experience and knowledge), reference power (evidenced by the degree of admiration felt towards the leader), and power for possession of information (the access the leader has to the sources of information that facilitate the achievement of the objectives). Later, we will see that some of these are more appropriate to ascend in the transpersonal leadership ladder.

Types of power

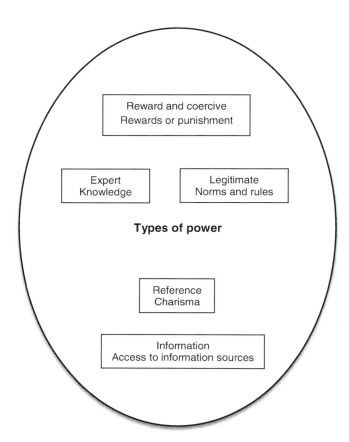

"The true test of a leader is if his followers adhere to their cause by their own free will, enduring arduous difficulties without being obliged to do so and remaining steadfast in the moments of greatest danger."

Xenophon

3. Promoting and facilitating the development of people and of the organization

The third step, promoting and facilitating followers and organizational development, provides a sense of direction to the actions of the leader. The leader, in this step, thinks primarily of the people and the organization, be this a family, a community or a country, when acting in the leadership role. Leaders who reach this step understand that their work is to facilitate the discovery of people's potential, without losing sight that this development should be intrinsically related to the organization to which they belong. In this step, the leader moves toward a people-focused and organizational-focused orientation. This step was perhaps the most developed in the bibliography of the 80s when it was popularized through the concept of Servant Leadership.

Leadership, at this stage, includes two processes that, in our view, lead to the true concept of democracy. These processes are empowerment and shared decision-making. They are grounded on a leader's valuation of followers as persons capable of making decisions and effectively contribute to the socio-organizational processes in which they are involved. Empowerment and shared decision making, two interlocked processes, relate to a leader's internalized respect for others. Empowerment is the recognition that people, regardless of their preparation, education, and personal characteristics, are able to contribute to social processes, to actions, and to results appropriately. It has to do with giving power (empowering) to people so they leave the follower role to become active collaborators who participate in the decision-making processes.

Empowerment

Empowerment reminds us the 1970's John Lennon song "Power to the People." Empowerment means to give people the power to intervene actively in the process of leadership. In this third stage of leadership development, promoting and facilitating the development of people and of the organization, empowerment means that the leader and collaborators can play different leadership roles, and that followers transform into collaborators. A visual way to describe empowerment in leadership is by recalling the scene in the film Gladiator when the leader asked his soldiers to march at his side - not behind him, not separated from him - and to make a great row in which each one is in contact with one another.

Empowerment means that the leader decides, consciously, to give power to the followers. In this process, ideas, opinions, and points of view are accepted, promoted, and facilitated by the leader. Giving people power promotes people's development. Followers who intervene in decision-making are better prepared to make future decisions and to take new actions, are more prone to implement the decisions, and feel more compromise with each other and with the organization. It is like the parent who lets his or her child solve a problem, avoiding telling him or her how to do it, or what steps to take, only giving small hints and clues. This is a way of empowering and educating for future interdependence. Empowerment closely relates to leader's confidence and certainty in his or her followers' ability to take right actions. In this point, distinguishing between faith and confidence is fundamental for transpersonal leadership. Additionally, the understanding of these differences is key for followership development.

Faith involves believing in something or someone, based on an emotional, not factual explanation. We believe because, within ourselves, there is "something" that tells us to believe. It is in this dimension where we decide to accept the existence of God, or where we believe in someone without data or information about that person's behavior. This dimension may be associated with a leader's reference power and charisma; people follow the leader because of something-- usually emotions and feelings tell them to do so. They have faith. People believe the leader will do what he or she says without evidence or expressed behaviors that prove it.

Confidence is the intermediate dimension of trust. People are confident in a leader because he or she has shown, on several occasions, to be reliable, and because they have some sympathetic feelings toward him or her. It is a mixture of emotions and feelings, with facts and evidence. Confidence accompanied with more facts and evidence, in repeated situations, leads progressively to certainty. In this level of trust people and their leader are transparent, honest and open in their relationship.

Certainty has to do with complete trust in the leader's performance because he or she has repeatedly been consistent and has acted in the way he or she says so. It is the dimension in which, without any doubt, people know how the leader will act in the future. Certainty results from the assessment of previous and current leader's behaviors. Collaborators develop certainty about a leader depending on what he or she does and has done. Certainty about the leader grows when collaborators learn that he or she is reliable, when they have positive experiences with him or her, and when their suppositions of the leader's behavior are fulfilled. People also develop certainty about a leader because they identify with him.

In the same way, leaders may have faith, feel confident, or have certainty for their collaborators. Leaders develop these feeling when collaborators repeatedly behave in the way leaders expect to.

Empowerment has to do with the leader's conviction that his or her collaborators will act in the appropriate way having witnessed repeatedly collaborators' appropriate behaviors. Empowerment occurs when the leader places the ability to decide in the hands of others and gives them the power to do what is needed. Empowering others is recognizing that each person has the potential to become a leader, and that leadership is not "something" that is innate, but something that people can develop with the right opportunities.

Empowerment puts the decision-making process in the hands of leader's collaborators. The leader understands that followers, in the future, will take leadership positions, and becomes a collaborator's mentor-tutor and coach to help them to reach higher levels of personal, professional, ethical, and moral development. Empowerment is directly related to shared-decision making, moving followers from passive participation to active intervention in planning and implementing their actions. Empowerment relates to Bass and Avolio's Transformational Leadership work, in 1994, and McGregor Burns' Transformative Leadership work, in 2003. At this point, we ask you, what leaders, known by you, have empowered their followers? Can you think of somebody who empowers you? How did he or she do so? Would you like to be like him or her?

Shared decision-making

Shared decision-making moves leadership and leaders from "few are right" to "everybody can contribute." It is based on inquiring about collaborators' opinions. It involves thinking of collaborators as people able to decide which actions to take. Shared decision making and empowerment provide a true sense of democracy. When leaders and collaborators make decisions together, confidence and respect among them increase as well. Promoting shared-decision making involves recognition and understanding of the diversity and the value of diverse opinions and points of view. Although shared decision-making can take more time than unilateral decision-making, it brings in a synergistic power that ensures decision implementation and good feeling and satisfaction among collaborators.

The promotion of shared-decision making implies that leaders move toward high levels of understanding and towards respect of his or her followers. Indeed, it entails seeing each person, not as a follower, but as a collaborator. Shared-decision making itself leads to collaborators' empowerment. The leader that actively promotes it is sending a message of "I trust you; I know you have the skills, and I know that we together can make a better decision than the one that I would make alone." This approach has some beneficial spin-offs. It allows contributors to do the following:

- test their competencies
- compare and confront their ideas with others' ideas,
- know how well aligned are their ideas with the organizational objectives
- know their peers and themselves better
- take part in the development of their organization
- increase their identification with fellow contributors, the leader, and the organization
- enhance their participation in the implementation of the decision
- increase their self-concept and self-esteem
- create a spirit of team and membership

Shared decision making goes far beyond consultation; it implies the leader actively facilitating collaborators' participation so that they become involved in the making and implementation of decisions. The leader who wants to increase shared decision-making must be aware of the different personalities of their collaborators' personalities... The leader must identify the collaborators who are introverts or extroverts, who are rational or emotional, who are conservatives or initiators, who see the events as cause and effect phenomena or as in intricate set of relations. The leader must know who are more oriented toward people and who to the tasks, who want to control and who wish to be controlled, who need structure and who do not. The leader who has this knowledge can promote each person's involvement at different times, in different issues, depending on the dynamics of the decision-making process and the type of decisions to be made. In addition, the leader who is able to promote diverse participation can obtain different points of view and different angles on the same subject; as a result, the chance of success in each decision increases.

Democratic attitude

Leaders who want to develop their collaborators should cultivate a democratic attitude. This highlights behaviors of respect for different opinions regardless of who proposed them. A democratic attitude also promotes respect for the minority opinion, and respect for collaborators' differences in terms of their styles and ways of behaving. A democratic attitude goes beyond promoting people's participation in the decision-making process; it has to do with the acceptance of the dissimilarities of the groups that compose the organization and with the behaviors that promote the free expression of ideas. It has to do with the equal treatment of the collaborators, and with the consideration of the collaborators as human beings who have different interests. Finally, a democratic attitude is the foundation of the true transpersonal leader, who sees democracy as a sociopolitical structure where common goals and objectives appointed by groups with different ideas converge to produce the holistic development of people, the organization, and society.

A democratic attitude in leadership implies that leaders are aware of the effect of their actions on the collaborators, the organization, the community, and society. Leaders need to think soundly about what they say and do. They have to be aware of the consequences of their actions. A democratic attitude calls for an ability to be empathetic - to understand and place oneself in another's' position - especially in the positions of those who have diverging viewpoints. Leaders must display a democratic attitude that demonstrates the fact that they may not see what others can.

Finally, a democratic attitude in transpersonal leadership requires the leaders' ability to put their ego aside, even after having arrived at decisions they believe appropriate for the followers and the organization. In other words, a democratic attitude calls for a "reflective active-doubt", a type of thinking that requires leaders continually review their decisions without paralyzing themselves from taking actions. Because reflective-active-doubt is difficult, we believe that many people categorized as leaders are not transpersonal leaders. A democratic attitude takes the leader to the next level of leadership, from a self-centered attitude to a socio- centered one. Leaders with a socio-centered attitude see their collaborators, themselves, and the leadership actions as subordinate to society. Society becomes the center of the leadership.

Can you think of leaders who empower people, use a shared-decision making style, and have a democratic attitude? Please, keep these names in your mind.

Summary

The third step, promoting and facilitating the development of people and the organization, provides a sense of direction to leaders' actions. Leaders focus on people and on the organization. In this step, leadership has to do with empowerment, shared decision-making and democratic attitude.

Empowerment means giving power to people and changing their role from them from followers to collaborators, so they actively intervene in the leadership process. The leader and the collaborators are certain that everybody is able to undertake socially desirable actions.

Shared decision-making moves leadership from "a few are right" to "everyone can contribute." Shared decision-making is possible when leaders understands and respects their collaborators, and when leaders encourage them to intervene in the decision-making process.

A democratic attitude highlights respect for the views of the collaborators as well as their differences. Leaders are aware of how their behaviors affect his or her collaborators, other groups, organizations, or other segments of society. Additionally, a democratic attitude in transpersonal leadership implies a socio-centered orientation instead of an ego-centered one, and a reflective doubt.

Transpersonal Leadership

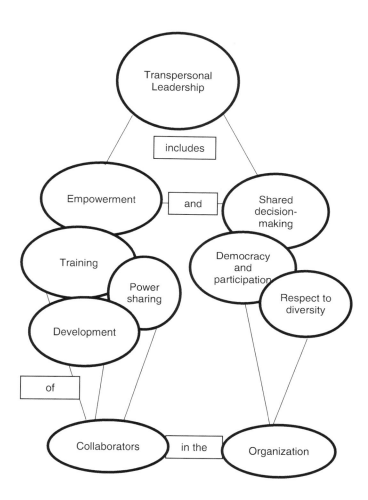

"You have to look at leadership through the eyes of the followers and you have to live the message. What I have learned is that people become motivated when you guide them to the source of their own power and when you make heroes out of employees who personify what you want to see in the organization."

Anita Roddick

4. Developing and practicing a socio-centered approach

In the fourth step, developing and practicing a socio-centered orientation, leaders act with the desire to serve society and not with the desire to be served by it. They do not want to be the center of everybody's attention. A socio-centered orientation moves leaders' thoughts outside the boundaries of the organization, as they understand that their actions influence the organization, the immediate environment, the community and society. In addition, a socio-centered orientation rests on leaders' abilities to act on behalf of others and to put aside their desire to be the fundamental factor of the leadership process. At this stage, leaders and collaborators define a pro-social organization's objectives and goals to favor society. They go beyond the organization, projecting their actions into the community and in other contexts. In this step, leaders see themselves as part of society and understand that social well-being mandates their organizational actions. This step moves the leader orientation from focused on the ego and the organization to a society-centered orientation. It is on this platform where the stewardship and servant leadership are placed. It is in this step where Mother Teresa and Gandhi, among others, can be set.

At this point, we want to address some questions to you: who, of those you consider leaders, have reached this step? How can you practice, in terms of behaviors, a socio-centered orientation? What organization, community and social leaders would you place in this step?

In the next paragraphs, we hope to help you find the answers to these questions. To this end, it is necessary to establish some ideas associated with a socio-centered orientation.

From the ego, the organization, the community, the society, the country, that brings us to...

The fourth step of leadership has two fundamental implications for the leader. First, leaders learn that they are but one of the many factors involved in the leadership process. Second, they deeply understand that social development is the peak goal of leadership. In this section, we discuss these implications.

The leader who has reached the fourth step, as it was pointed above, moves toward a socio-centered orientation, his or her actions and behaviors are not guided by his or her desire to be admired or to be perpetuated as an "icon of leadership" but are guided by social interests. Perhaps the best description of a socio-centric leader, in the family context, is the father or mother who does everything possible to raise good, ethical, independent children, and who are able to understand the value of interdependence, and able to manage their lives within a social context without expecting to get back anything from it. These parents, when old, do not expect their children take care of them or provide them with benefits. These parents know that their children are more important than they are. They know their children belong to society.

Leaders, at this stage, see organizations as entities where there is something more than a working relationship; they see the organization as a fundamental form of social arrangement. In other words, the leader considers organizational purposes more important than personal purposes and understands that it is within organizations where people reach personal and social accomplishments and where people benefit from their achievements. The leader knows that people-organization interdependencies produce mutual benefits. The leader, collaborators, and the organization give to and receive from each other something desirable for all. Leaders who are moderately aware of their roles, in this stage of development, guide their actions and behaviors toward the well-being of the community. They understand that their role as a leader goes beyond the organizational environment and that the organization is part of a broader context, in which pro-social actions should produce benefits for all. In this sense, the leader emphasizes that organizational effectiveness needs to be measured by including parameters related to the well-being of the immediate community where the organization operates. A leader develops positive personal, social, legal, ethical and moral criteria related to organizational processes and products to avoid harming the community. In addition, the leader comprehends that organizations have to deal with business, earnings, and social responsibility, so he or she actively promotes these through personal and community development programs addressed to increase everybody's well-being.

Leaders who are highly aware of their roles, in this step of development, understand that they are part of an organization, and the organization is part of the community and part of the society. He or she understands that his or her actions and behaviors should properly impact the community where the organization operates and should impact also society, which must receive some of the organization's profits in the form of jobs, streets, sidewalks, public lighting, people's growth, citizenship development, environmental conservation awareness programs, social identity programs, cultural development activities, and social diversity appreciating.

The leader who has arrived at this step knows the network of interrelations that exist between organizational and social systems. He or she knows that any action performed to improve the organization could have positive or negative effects on society. Additionally, he or she knows that social development is as important as organizational development, because organizations are open systems that receive input from society, some of which are very concrete such as human capital, technologies, regulations and laws or as intangible as ideas, culture, creeds and social philosophies, and, in turn, send products back to it. The leader at this stage should align the organization's identity with societal expectations and understand that increasing organizational effectiveness and social betterment are fundamental elements of the leadership process.

The second fundamental implication, valuing the organization and society, has to do with the development of ethical and moral organizations and societies where democracy and people's participation are the paragons, and where leaders and collaborators use their knowledge and wisdom in favor of others. This relates directly to the empowerment of constituents. In this point, we believe it is necessary to describe some different social and organizational structures, such as prescriptive, entrepreneur and knowledge. These structures bring different responses from leaders and collaborators.

Organizations and societies

Leaders - who have ascended to the fourth step, developing and practicing a socio-centered orientation - need to promote the creation of knowledge organizations and societies, in which people use information and develop knowledge, in creative ways, to benefit others. We believe that it is important to describe some social arrangements that relate to the development of transpersonal leadership. These include prescriptive, entrepreneurial, and knowledge organizations and societies. We are aware of the fact that these do not exhaust all structure-functioning forms of organizations; however, we found them appropriate for the discussion of transpersonal leadership.

Prescriptive organization/society

Prescriptive organizations and societies are reactive, cautious, hierarchical and centralized. These features allow us to create a profile of the leader's role in this type of organization and social structures. The leader who supports prescriptive organizations and societies believe that people's behaviors should be rewarded or punished depending on predefined performance criteria. He or she believes that he or she should wait that things happen to correct or institutionalize them. He or she avoids taking risks because testing new ideas not prescribed or established is not right. The leader, in these organizational and social structures, considers people as subordinates who must follow orders and who must not suggest different and new ways to solve problems because the solutions are already prescribed. Consequently, the leader looks for means to maintain the control of processes, especially those that have to do with decision-making.

Prescriptive organizations and societies have cultural characteristics that are appropriate when contextual changes are minimal or absent, and when they operate in a placid-controlled environment. Some of these cultural characteristics include the use of logic to make decisions, formal and mechanistic structures, a clear and limited definition of members' roles and functions, stability through regulations, norms, and laws to guide people's behaviors. In a prescriptive organization/society, if something is not regulated, it is not appropriate and, therefore, negative.

Additionally, prescriptive organizations and societies characterize by their high sensitivity to people's status and position, both of which are legitimized by the regulations and standards and the use of legitimate power. These organizations and societies suppress conflict because is negative, denying the learning and knowledge associated with it. They search for efficiency - achieving the maximum with the minimum cost - with partial or no consideration or analysis of the potential impact of new internal and external organizational elements and factors. These characteristics constitute weaknesses when the organizations operate in changing, turbulent and global contexts. Culture in prescriptive organizations and societies rests on order, rules, uniformity, and pre-established standards. These parameters may be appropriate, as we have pointed out above, in placid and stable environments, where changes occur at a very low rate and where the development of new processes and ideas could, wrongly, be deemed unnecessary.

Leaders in prescriptive organizations and societies direct and command. They guide and order people's participation if it exists. They inhibit new ways of proceeding, especially if they come from subordinates. These leaders believe themselves to have a "clear vision" of what is and who is right--people have to do what and how the leader says. At this point, we leave you with a question to think about, how can you characterize your organization and society? Which of those characteristics are encouraged by leaders you know?

Entrepreneurial organization/society

Entrepreneurial organizations and societies are proactive, intuitive, willing to take risks, and centralized. In entrepreneurial organizations and societies, people do not wait for things to happen--they actively promote it. Sometimes, the mechanisms used to make decisions fall outside the canons of "rationality"; for example, leaders could encourage the use of people's experiences and intuition, which may not be easily describable and reproducible, to make decisions. The leader promotes innovation and risk-taking to do things differently or to undertake actions using unconventional models. These organizations and societies, although clearly differentiated from prescriptive societies, preserve centralization as a way to keep control.

Cultural characteristics of entrepreneurial organizations and societies include a mix of new aspects with elements of the prescriptive ones. Entrepreneurial organizations and societies search for functionality – doing things following a previously defined purpose. They are organic, which provides a certain range of freedom to integrate new ways of decision-making and administration functions in their day-to-day operations. They search for stability while responding to environmental changes to balance previously established and "adequate ways" with novel ideas and methods. They regard collaboration, discipline, compromise, and dedication as the fundamental values for achieving organizational results. In these organizations and societies, the leader becomes a permanent motivator of collaborators, sometimes with a negative consequence; collaborators develop preference for external motivators and incentives.

Leaders in entrepreneurial organizations and societies consider discipline essential to achieve organizational results. As is the case in prescriptive organizations and societies, entrepreneurial organizations and societies are sensitive to status. Roles and functions are critical, and people must predefine their actions and their achievements. In addition, entrepreneurial organizations and societies look for efficiency, minimum cost and maximum achievement, which is essential for them. Just as in the prescriptive organizations, in entrepreneurial organizations and societies, the leaders seek control through rules but recognize that rules will depend on contextual characteristics. Finally, entrepreneurial organizations and societies function properly in placid-casual environments, which characterize by a relative stability and some predictable changes that allow organizations to re-define their goals. In these environments, leaders and collaborators can discern the causes of variations easily.

In entrepreneurial organizations and societies, the leader stands out as a director-consultant. He or she looks for collaborators' participation after providing some ideas and options, from which supporters "select" one or some of those options that the leader may or may not accept. In addition, the leader thinks that only those who are "suitable" can intervene and participate in the decision-making process. Undoubtedly, this presupposes that "common people" who have not achieved certain competencies or positions considered desirable, have no opportunity to get involved in the decision-making processes. As an example of this, you may recall when in the past, because of some rules, only men who had learned to read and write could vote. These rules left uneducated citizens and women excluded. Can you say that those people who could not vote were incompetent to define their socio-political future just because they were not educated or were female?

Finally, in entrepreneurial organizations and societies, the leader promotes the participation of others but he or she is the one who ultimately approves the participants' ideas thereafter. This kind of behavior is displayed by governments and organizations whose leaders are surrounded by technocrats and consultants who make decisions based on technical issues without considering, in many cases, sociocultural factors - labeled frequently as "technically inappropriate" and "subjective," and without seeing unanticipated/undesirable consequences.

Knowledge organization/society

Knowledge organizations and societies are different from prescriptive and entrepreneurial ones. They are highly orientated toward problem solving and decision-making. In these, the leader use methods that activate collaborators' participation and the awareness that change is a permanent, prevalent need.

In knowledge organizations and societies, constant change is the response to continuous environmental and contextual transformations. The leader, in these organizations, far from maintaining the status quo, actively stimulates change to keep the organization adapting to new requests and working effectively. Knowledge organizations and societies recognize the value of rationality, intuition, and individuality. For this reason, their leaders seek out collaborators' behavioral preferences and personality differences to set them in the most appropriate context. The leader who recognizes collaborators' individuality respects their backgrounds and behaviors and opposes promoting a set of predetermined "desirable" ones.

In knowledge organizations and societies, people, social dynamic and organizational characteristics empower collaborators to make decisions with a teamwork orientation. Teams - including people from different specialties, with different behavioral preferences, working around a task and pursuing decisions based on diverse viewpoints – are one of the most important factors in knowledge organizations and societies to function effectively.

Knowledge organizations and societies tend to decentralization. Decentralization, within the transpersonal leadership framework, signifies shared responsibility, valuing of each organizational entity, and recognition of individual and contextual differences. Decentralization also implies that all people are interdependently responsible for the choices they make, whether because they actively engage in those choices or because they avoid commitment and leave others to decide for them. Finally, an essential element of knowledge organizations and societies is that the coordination of tasks is achieved through dialogue, which moves the leader from the level of superiority to one of equality, where all stakeholders have the same possibility to intervene and decide on matters affecting them.

The characteristics set out above, in relation to knowledge societies and organizations, bring as result the development of a flexible culture, oriented toward problem-solving, decision-making, critical thinking, and creativity. Organizations and societies open to new forms of behavior, to new creeds and philosophies directly related to effectiveness, and to processes addressed to get the best results have an enduring positive impact on leaders and stakeholders.

Control, in knowledge organizations and societies, is based on information and knowledge to solve problems, not on rules and regulations. Rules are set to help people recognize the elements and relationships of existing systems and environments involved in the social or organizational design. In addition, laws and rules are general and contextual. They are guiding principles that are adapted to the situation. These principles are meant to facilitate people's proper behaviors instead of prescriptions intended to determine what people should do. This view has a direct relationship to the perception of change as a permanent process where people have the freedom to create new ways within general parameters, and to today's globalized organizations and societies operating in turbulent environments, which demand from leaders and collaborators varying and new behaviors to respond to changing contexts.

The appropriate type of leadership in knowledge organizations and societies is transpersonal leadership, which is characterized by the acceptance of people as they are and by the understanding of their positions without judgment. Transpersonal leaders approach relations in terms of the present, not the past, treat those close to them and the stranger with the same courteous and attentive manner. Transpersonal leaders, trust collaborators and act without seeking approval and recognition from others. Transpersonal leadership, as Transformational leadership, an approach pointed by Bass and Avolio in their book *Transformational Leadership in Organizations*, includes the inspiration of collaborators through ideas, the motivation, the intellectual stimulation, and the consideration of the uniqueness of each person as fundamental elements. It is because of these elements that transpersonal leaders use referent power and idealist persuasion to influence collaborators.

In knowledge organizations and societies, the leader develops and practices of a socio-centric orientation, rejects his or her personal interests, and becomes a public servant. These leaders make fundamental changes in the organizations and societies they belong to and place social well-being as the ultimate purpose of their actions. Some reflection is necessary at this point: how do you define the society to which you belong? Which of the leaders who you know have a socio-centered attitude? Do those leaders have a clear concept of what is a knowledge organization and society? Your next step is to place your organizations, your community, your country, and your leaders in one of these formats. Leaders should display socio-centered behaviors in knowledge organizations and societies, and they must practice those very beyond their immediate surroundings, in global contexts. These premises lead us to the next level of leadership, practicing a global and ecological orientation.

Summary

The fourth step, developing and practicing a socio-centric orientation, moves leaders' actions outside of the organizational boundaries, and outside of their immediate environments. Leaders and collaborators define organizational purposes, without losing sight that those purposes must have positive consequences for society. Leaders move from self-centeredness to socio-centeredness, from focusing on themselves to focusing on the society.

In this step, leaders understand that social well-being is the guiding principle of their actions. They conceive social change as the norm and promote the conversion of the organization and the society into one of knowledge. Additionally, they promote the development of a flexible culture oriented toward problem solving, decision-making, critical thinking, and creativity.

The leader, in this step, becomes Transpersonal when he or she accepts people as they are, trusts in them, approaches relationships in terms of present, and inspires collaborators.

The leader who reaches the fourth step becomes a true "public servant" who effectively balances personal, organizational, and social interests.

From ego-centrism to socio-centrism

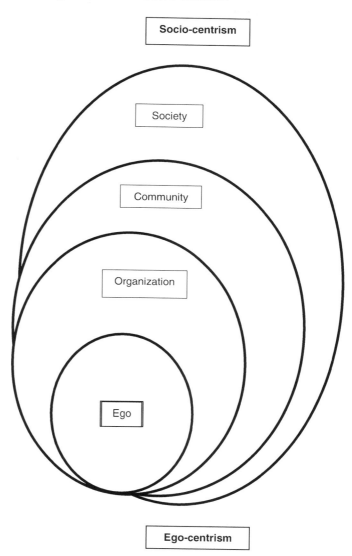

"Men make history and not the other way around. In periods where there is no leadership, society stands still. Progress occurs when courageous, skillful leaders seize the opportunity to change things for the better."

Harry Truman

5. Practicing a global and ecological orientation

The fifth and last step of transpersonal leadership is practicing a global and ecological orientation, which comprises the highest level of leadership development. In this context, ecological orientation is based on the ideas of Bronfenbrenner expressed in his 1979 article, *Social-Ecological Model for Human Development:* humans develop through different systems; each system contains roles, norms, and rules that may shape their psychological development, moving from micro systems such as family to social macro systems. An ecological orientation has also to do with the acquisition of a global consciousness, whereby the leader's actions influence and are influenced by people, communities, cultures, and countries. In this step, the leader leaves the local environment to move into a global environment. In addition, acting ecologically also means, in addition to having an environmental awareness, possessing the wisdom to understand and respect other people and their social identities, viewpoints, cultures, creeds, and ideas.

The fifth step also refers to valuing diversity and looking out for people's well-being, regardless of their origin and ethnicity. It is being "globally empathetic" before making decisions that can seem beneficial to their local environment. In short, leaders who practice a global and ecological orientation understand that our planet includes different groups and that their roles contribute to the well-being of the people throughout the world and to the well-being of the planet.

The leader, in this fifth stage, should recognize and respect diversity among people and social groups. Recognition of diversity implies leaders' understanding of people's different points of view, attitudes, and ideas. The difference between this step and the previous step, developing and practicing a socio-centric orientation, is that now the leader's consciousness takes a global dimension. These leaders recognize diversity in their local, regional, and global contexts. They understand that societies have different customs, religions, convictions, and philosophies, which do not make them good or bad, simply different. The leaders who have reached this step practice a "global empathy" which allows them to step into the "shoes" of other social groups.

The second element, respect for people's differences, is a consequence of acknowledging diversity. Leaders who reach the fifth step know that other people's opinions are as valuable as theirs are, and that differences should be resolved through dialogue and debate based on global principles defined and adopted by all those who have interests in the issue.

In the fifth step, the leader becomes a concerned "inhabitant of the planet" and takes actions that are suitable for everyone and not only for his or her social group or country. When leaders reach this step, everyone, regardless of their nationality, supports their actions. Mother Theresa, Mandela, and Gandhi reached this step and most people recognize them as universal leaders. The fifth step is the peak of leadership development.

At this point, we propose some questions for you to reflect on: do you know leaders who think globally? What must leaders do to achieve this global and ecological position? Can a person claim to be a global leader without having reached the previous steps? Do you know leaders who have reached this level? Having some leaders' names in mind, what would you call them: leaders in the first step, third step or fifth step? Finally, and perhaps the most challenging question, where, in which step, would you place Castro, Hitler, Carter, Napoleon, Bolivar, Putin, Obama, Walesa, and Trump?

Final consideration about fifth step leadership

In this section, we lay out some final considerations regarding the fifth step leadership. We believe these considerations will give you a clearer idea about what leaders who have reached this step do. The leader who reaches this step, the highest level of leadership development, acts in the following ways

• Takes risks not taken over by others
• Creates an atmosphere of excellence, for the people, the organization, the society, and the planet
• Uses information and knowledge to solve problems and make decisions
• Empowers people, teaching them how to learn
• Provides opportunities for people to access and use information and knowledge

The Transpersonal leader, one who is in the fifth step, believes that knowledge organizations and societies are the best forms of social interaction; therefore, he or she actively undertakes the following actions:

• Establishes mechanisms for the acquisition of information
• Creates models of dissemination of information
• Provides tools that allow people to interpret information

• Encourages the use of information and knowledge to solve situations and make decisions
• Facilitates integration of new and current knowledge in new contexts
• Creates processes and "spaces" to store knowledge
• Democratizes knowledge

Leaders who have reached this level of growth know that learning and development, two processes that empower people, are essentials for promoting personal and social well-being. Therefore, they conceive learning and development as an organized and systematic process that implies learning about social and organizational-structural factors and contextual rules, information and knowledge management, principles and values socially accepted, and meta-learning - learning to learn.

In the scheme of learning to learn, Transpersonal leaders should push collaborators through various types of learning: acquiring data and information, analyzing critically the data and the information, relating data and information to problem solution and knowledge building, and understanding, developing, applying knowledge, assessing knowledge and using knowledge to achieve pro-social goals. The consequence of this scheme of learning is collaborators' personal and social development, personal independence, and social interdependence.

Fifth-level leaders, the transpersonal leaders, facilitate the rise of collaborators towards high levels of personal, professional, and social development. These leaders want collaborators to have a problem-solution and decision-making attitude. They want collaborators to be able to analyze and select the best alternative using multiple perspectives, to develop critical thinking by promoting the understanding of the meaning of their actions and the implications, and to develop creative thinking by taking risks and developing ideas and new products even if they deviate from the accepted ways of action. Additionally, they want collaborators to be able to develop their leadership potential by becoming pro-social change agents and socially oriented leaders, to recognize when to withdraw their support to a leader who has moved towards selfish-personal purposes, and to criticize leaders' actions when needed.

The fifth level leader, the transpersonal leader, empowers people and encourages them to seek new relationships both within their own community and with other communities; the transpersonal leader recognizes the value of partnerships and therefore stimulates them. He or she promotes knowledge and information exchange to solve problems in social environments. This leader communicates and teaches people the value of accessing and using information and knowledge to solve problems and reach further political, social, and economic development. The Transpersonal leader empowers society when he or she provides members with information and knowledge to change prescriptive organizations and societies into ones of knowledge. The Transpersonal leader empowers people so that they become transformation agents and starring characters in the development of their communities, helping them to become leaders.

Transpersonal leaders use debates and dialogues to reach decisions. Using plural values and principles and people's competencies (abilities, skills, knowledge, attitudes) within ethical and moral parameters defined through critical thinking processes - develops in his or her collaborators the need to debate and dialogue in a socialized fashion to reach decisions in our globalized and turbulent environments.

Transpersonal leadership is a novel concept of leadership. It goes beyond influencing followers. It is transforming collaborators into agents of change. It is facilitating people's development of diversity recognition, pro-social values and ethics in a global world. The meanings of prosocial values and ethical foundations in transpersonal leadership are developed in the next section.

Summary

The fifth step, practicing a global and ecological orientation is the highest level in the development of a leader. A leader at this step attains a global consciousness and understands that his or her actions influence people, communities, and countries. In other words, in this step, the leader becomes "globally empathetic." In addition, an ecological orientation means respecting people, societies and their cultures, and understanding and valuing diversity, regardless of people ethnicity, origin, or characteristics.

The two main elements of the fifth step of transpersonal leadership are the recognition of diversity and respect for individuals and differences among social groups; these elements include the acceptance of culture, religion, customs, creeds and philosophical differences, while being recognizably pro-social.

Transpersonal leadership, in this step, relates closely to dialogue and to the development of global principles - defined by and adopted with the participation of all people, organizations, communities, societies, and countries - to helping people behave within a planetary frame of reference.

Fifth stair leadership

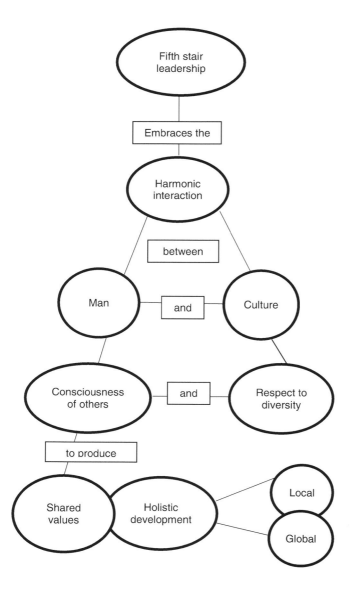

"Enlightened leadership is spiritual if we understand spirituality not as some kind of religious dogma or ideology but as the domain of awareness where we experience values like truth, goodness, beauty, love and compassion, and also intuition, creativity, insight and focused attention."

Deepak Chopra

6. Ethics and Transpersonal leadership

A discussion about leadership would be incomplete if it does not include ethics in leadership. Recent scandals of corruption around the world seem to be seeping in all spheres of public and private power, including presidents of nations, bankers, politicians, business people, military, and monarchs. Just look at the national and international press to corroborate these facts. Still, education, one of our most precious treasures, reflects the same trend. Beck (2000) established that the use of drugs, teenage pregnancy, and juvenile delinquency are, even today, events that call for a review of the moral and ethical dimension of leadership. In 1998, Bass and Steidlmeiner pointed that ethics is a dimension of leadership that had been little studied. Later, in 2006, Brown and Treviño, in their book *Ethical Leadership: A Review of Future Directions* established that ethics is an element that differentiates leaders from pseudo-leaders.

Brown and Treviño explored the meaning of ethical leadership and found a large number of personality traits related to it. People perceive ethical leaders as honest, reliable, fair decision makers, people with principles, concerned for others and for the society, with altruistic motivations and ethical behavior in their personal and professional lives.

In this same order of ideas, when we asked the more than 700 attendees of our workshops on leadership development what characterized a leader, most of the responses related to the ethical dimension of leadership and included attributes such as integrity, understanding of others' values, commitment, empathy, honesty, and responsibility. The vast majority of participants, which included people from education, military, business, insurance, and manufacturing, included the characteristics honesty, moral integrity, and ethics. Ethics, one of the least studied and publicly expressed features on leadership, is one of the characteristics people expressed leaders should possess.

Another aspect revealed by Brown and Treviño, named the "Moral Dimension of the Manager", relates to people who "make of ethics an explicit agenda of its leadership by communicating values and ethical messages, modeling visible and intentionally ethical behavior, and using a system of rewards to reinforce followers' responsibility" (p. 596). In other words, ethical leaders show consistency between their principles and ethical and moral values and the way they practice these principles. In the same order of ideas, Amat found that consistent behavior – "I do what I say" – is an attribute displayed among effective university leaders. Ethics and morality are underlying concerns in leadership seminars and workshops, for this reason, we think it is worth their inclusion in the discussion about transpersonal leadership. Nevertheless, before going there, please, think about those whom you see as leaders and decide whether they are leaders or pseudo leaders as based on their ethical behavior.

Ethics is a part of the philosophy that deals with human morals and obligations. This definition limits ethics to morality and responsibility - what must be done. In the same token, Solomon and Hanson in their book *Above the Bottom Line: An Introduction to Business Ethics* (1983), establish that ethics is, above all, the understanding of what is good to live rightly and to have a life that is worth living. They see ethics as a matter of perspectives that involves setting each personal activity and purpose in the "right place" and knowing what is, and what is not, valuable to love, to have and to do. Then, personal ethics is the blueprint, the map of good behaviors for living a good life. Additionally, Hitt and Pastin talk about ethical systems, defining them as a set of values related to the people's preferred modes of behavior to make the right decisions. Hitt, in 1990, in his book *Ethics and Leadership* says that an ethical system is a group of interrelated values. Pastin in 1984, considers that a system of ethics is the set of rules and principles to make correct decisions.

Thus, ethical systems include values, principles, and rules that guide people's behaviors and decision-making processes. These values, principles, and rules should serve to benefit people, organizations, and the society. The problem is how do we know if a person, a leader, is doing what is right, what is good, what should be done? A discussion about types of ethics might give us a better perspective to make decisions.

Most of the choices people make could be analyzed from four perspectives:

• Results should provide the maximum benefit at the minimum cost.
• The law establishes what must be done and how it must be done.
• The organization, community, and society set the values, and principles that must be followed.
• Convictions and conscience guide people's actions.

These four descriptions represent what Hitt, in the 90s, called the systems of ethics. The first perspective leads to ethics based on goals and results, proposed by John Stuart, who established that moral behaviors are determined by its consequences and outcomes. The second relates to ethics based on laws, rules, and regulations, proposed by Kant. The third perspective has to do with ethics based on the social contract, proposed by Rousseau, who established that moral behaviors are determined by the customs, values, principles, and standards of an organization, community, or society. The fourth perspective is framed into the personal ethics proposed by Martin Ruber, who advocated that the individual's conscience determines what is morally right.

We summarize these four systems of ethics as:

- Result-dependent ethics,
- Legal-dependent ethics,
- Socio-dependent ethics, and
- Personal-dependent ethics.

The unthoughtful use of different systems of ethics by people is, perhaps, another factor that makes people deem Hitler, Mother Teresa, Churchill, Napoleon, Bolivar, and Christ, among others, as leaders. However, when we evaluate their social contribution, we find that definitively it was not the same, and in some cases, was even a negative one. We believe that these ethical systems will allow people to find a better approximation to define the ethics of leadership.

Parameters to evaluate decisions

In 2001, Thiroux and Krasemann, in their book *Ethics, Theory and Practice*, present a group of attributes that can help evaluate decisions. These attributes relate to the ethical systems. They established that a decision should:

- be rational but accompanied with emotionality.
- be logical but not rigid or inflexible.
- be universally applicable to humankind.
- be applicable to particular situations in a practical way.
- be likely to be taught and enacted.
- solve conflicts.
- include the duties and obligations of human beings.

We add to these attributes the necessity that a decision produces well-being for all.

Leaders make decisions considering different ethical systems. Those who consider the result-dependent system believe that the right thing to do is to maximize the "desirable" consequences of the decision. Leaders who consider the legal-dependent system argue that it is right to comply with the provisions of the law. Those who take a socio-dependent position think that what society deems as correct is right. Leaders who make decisions based on a personal-dependent system consider the right thing is what the person's conscience "says." In some cases, these systems overlap and people make decisions considering more than one system at a time. However, it is necessary to stress that the attributes: "be universally applicable to humankind and to particular situations in a practical way, solve conflicts, consider the duties and obligations of human beings, and produce the maximum well-being for all" are undisputable when leaders make decisions using any ethical system.

As previously expressed, decisions may not be limited to a single ethical system. We believe it is fundamental to ponder all systems when making a decision. We also believe that it is necessary for leaders and collaborators feel positive after making a decision. For this reason, it is appropriate to evaluate the decisions using the four ethical systems. The application of several systems of ethics by leaders does not guarantee that they have done the right thing and does not guarantee that they will feel good about the decision; however, it gives leaders and collaborators a theoretical support to understand better their actions.

Hitt establishes a strategy for deciding on situations that present profound ethical dilemmas. He says the person must approach the situation, first from a result-dependent point of view; then, continue with a legal-dependent; later, use a socio-dependent approach; and finally, use a personal-dependent point of view. This process involves the in-depth analysis of the situation from different perspectives, understanding the "pros" and "cons" in different contexts. However, at the end, two cardinal questions arise after a person, or a leader, has made a decision using Hitt's strategy, "Could I defend it before others and before myself? And, can I 'live' with it?"

Reflecting on the previous paragraph, ask yourself, can some of the people you see as leaders knowingly and correctly defend their decisions before the social group they are part of? In addition, do you think they can "live" with their decisions? Even if you use only one of the system of ethics or, more desirably, several of them, it is important to understand that the final decision is not made by the "system" but by a. As Hitt essentially puts it, the person's reasoning is what serves as the arbitrator to make the final decision.

Another reflection is essential here; can rationality be above convictions or vice versa? We believe that a "broad-minded" leader who confronts a difficult decision, which could lead to good or bad implications or even go against his or her "reasoning" and convictions, must decide based on what will produce well-being for all. In this way, he or she would affirm his or her true condition of a leader and would promote his or her growth by reviewing and even abandoning his or her beliefs when people's well-being is at stake.

At this point, we think you are in a better position to understand those debates about whether Hitler's actions were right or wrong or why some people say that they can understand his actions and position but not share it. It is possible that people who are discussing leadership and who is or is not a leader, are doing so using different systems of ethics as a result of having different ways of appreciating life, different backgrounds, and different experiences and expectations. However, we deeply believe that the inclusion of well-being for all, a mixture of end-results with social-contract ethics, is required to achieve transpersonal leadership. Do you think that well-being for all is the fundamental issue of leadership?

In this sense, Boatman (1997) posted some ethical principles that leaders must follow. They should conduct themselves in the following ways:

• Respect themselves and others' autonomy, without limiting people's freedom to choose.
• Treat all people as equals, being impartial and objective.
• Avoid damaging physical, emotional and psychologically him or herself and others.
• Be authentic, telling the truth, living up to their promises and acting consistently.
• Provide benefit, contributing to the well-being of all.

Ethical systems and democracy

These principles apply to Transpersonal leaders, and, at the same time, are directly aligned with democracy as a sociopolitical way of living, where the well-being and the participation of all those who make up the society are fundamental. We know that under this perspective, not all those called leaders truly are.

In the leadership ladder, the second step, influencing by appealing to moral and ethical principles, contemplates result-dependent and social-dependent ethical systems to produce well-being and benefit for all as the greatest values. The application of these systems of ethics to a global context can be set in the fifth and final step - practicing a global and ecological orientation – of transpersonal leadership. In this step, leaders understand how their actions influence and people, communities, cultures, and countries influence them. These systems of ethics are within the venue of a global orientation when people and societies understand and respect each other, and when they take into account all needs, views, cultures, creeds, and ideas before making decisions. Using globalized ethical systems to make decisions may be a medium to provide people of the world with the greatest possible benefit.

In short, the leader who recognizes all people's principles, values, and social needs, and practices an ethical, global, and ecological orientation contributes to world well-being. The leader becomes a "planetary leader" aimed at undertaking actions that are appropriate and socially desirable for everyone.

The ethics of transpersonal leadership rests on the idea that of the developing collaborators is inherently linked to people's pro socio-global shared purposes, which leads to personal, organizational, social and global well-being. Transpersonal leaders act ethically by encouraging critical thinking in their collaborators. They promote an understanding of their actions, and the implications derived from those actions, in terms of global benefits and social acceptance. In Transpersonal leadership collaborators, organizational and societal viewpoints and expectations are fundamental factors in making decisions that result in global well-being. In short, transpersonal leadership and ethics are indissoluble.

Is not the searching for global well-being an expression of a leader's ethical and moral conduct? What do you think?

Summary

Ethics is the part of the philosophy that studies moral obligations. It is a group of interrelated values referred to desirable modes of behavior and a set of rules and principles used to make right decisions. However, what is right? What is good? These questions are not easy to answer. Studying different systems of ethics could help us to answer these questions.

Most ethical choices fall into four ethical perspectives:
- Result-dependent
- Legal-dependent
- Socio-dependent
- Personal-dependent

Some characteristics related to the ethical systems, presented by Thiroux and Krasemann in 2001 may help evaluate our decisions. Decisions should include rationality, feelings, and emotions; decisions be logical and flexible; they should be universally applicable to humanity and to particular situations; they should be likely to be taught and enacted; decisions should solve conflicts and acknowledge the duties and obligations of human begins. In addition, we believe that a decision should produce the maximum well-being for all.
The application of one or several systems of ethics to make decisions does not guarantee having made the right thing and does not guarantee feeling good about that decision. However, ethical systems give us the theoretical support to better understand and guide leaders' actions and our own actions.

Ethics and Transpersonal leadership are interconnected. Transpersonal leaders act ethically when they encourage collaborators to think critically and understand the meaning and implications of their actions in terms of social acceptance and global benefits.

Ethics and Transpersonal Leadership

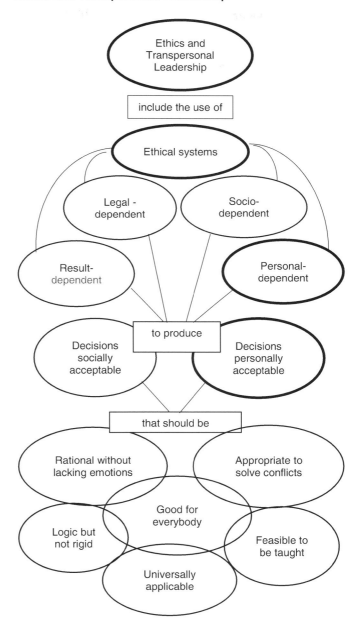

"The ethics of leadership rests on three pillars: the moral character of the leader, the ethical values of the leader that supporters embrace or reject and the morality of socio-ethical processes of the leader and his followers."

James McGregor Burns

7. Transpersonal Leadership

The term transpersonal means "beyond" personal, and refers to events, processes, and experiences that transcend our usual sense of identity, allowing us to experience a more complete and significant reality in terms of subjects, factors, relations, and variables involved. Daniels in his book *Sombra, Yo y Espiritu (Shadows, Spirit and I)*, Daniels (2008) suggests that human beings reach the transpersonal state when they transcend their individual senses and identify themselves with a greater awareness. This increased awareness and transcendence, in terms of transpersonal leadership, means that leaders should exhibit a positive social role and a socio-centered conception.

Transpersonal development goes through several developmental stages described in Wilber's development of consciousness model. Wilber's model contends that people's consciousness increases, going from lower to upper levels. In this model, a new level of consciousness, or step, would include and integrate the previous level of consciousness. The integration involves the development and internalization of new skills, knowledge, abilities, and attitudes. It involves learning. Transpersonal leaders do learn but gradually understand better their contexts. They take a systemic position about issues and events, and relate to people in different ways, fundamentally, they change from a personal, private, self-centered attitude to a social, socio-centered attitude, whose fundamental purpose is all people's well-being.

Understanding trans-personality entails understanding the conscious as a personal, social, and universal phenomenon. Wilber expressed that people reach the transpersonal level when they achieve and transcend to a higher level of consciousness; we call this, in transpersonal leadership, socio-universal consciousness. Similarly, Miller in 1998 called it trans-ego state, which is similar to a socio-centered attitude in transpersonal leadership.

Transpersonal leadership, as we said above, has to do with the development of prosocial values, with self-realization of the existence of different social, ethnic, cultural groups, and with everyone's right to a good life. This conception is similar to Maslow's higher level of motivation, the transcendence of the ego toward a social dimension, the unit of the being, the integrative consciousness, and the global synergy between individuals. Transpersonal leadership is a developmental process aligned with Transpersonal Psychology, which, as Stan Grof establishes in his book *La Psicologia del Futuro*

(The Psychology of the Future), focuses on the consciousness and the internal psychological development to find a transpersonal identity in connection with the community and the nature.

In Transpersonal leadership, the leader develops and promotes the progress of collaborators so they achieve social and global shared purposes, leading to personal, organizational, social and global well-being. In this sense, transpersonal leadership includes four key elements. The first relates to the transformation of a person into a socio-conscious human being, guided by moral and ethical elements, and by global and social principles that have the potential to produce benefits to society. The second element has to do with people's development towards higher levels of ethical and moral stages. These two elements are congruent with what Mc Gregor Burns, in his book *Leadership*, and Bass and Avolio, in his work *Improving Organizational Effectiveness: Through Transformational Leadership*, call Transforming and Transformational Leadership, respectively. However, transpersonal leadership goes beyond the social idea of these authors. The third element moves the leader out from power to influence, to produce change and to make decisions by him or herself to the interdependence leader-collaborator-context to do so. These three interdependent factors must intervene in the process of decision-making and change. The leader promotes development and change but, at the same time, recognizes that during this process people, including leaders themselves, should promote their own development and change. The fourth element implies the substitution of external incentives to stimulate desirable behaviors for the combination of external and internal motivators to do so, until the internal ones become collaborator's behavioral guides. It establishes that people are what their fellow human beings, communities, and societies have made out of them, and what each person has made out of him or herself. In synthesis, transpersonal leaders facilitate the transformation of people into global thinkers who practice ethics and moral globally defined, understand the relationship among them, the leader, and the context, and substitute external incentives to internal motivators. Transpersonal leaders achieve by:

• Supporting their own global socially acceptable ethical and moral development.
• Facilitating moral and ethical standards development in others.
• Changing the leadership process from power to influence to power to facilitate change.

• Including themselves, the collaborators, and the context in decision-making and changing processes.
• Moving people from the using of external incentives toward the using of internal motivators.
• Moving from "the ego" towards the organization and the society, combining personal, organizational, social, and global knowledge.
• Providing and promoting the creation of "significant" meanings in collaborators.

The following paragraphs describe in detail each of these features to help you to grasp more fully the concept of transpersonal leadership.

Supporting their own global socially acceptable ethical and moral development.

The Transpersonal leader is able to manage his or her personal and ethical development. Transpersonal leadership is achieved when the leader leads with ethical and moral principles, is social and globally accepted, and influences people keeping in mind their well-being and socio-ethical and moral principles.

Ethics and morals must be associated with social and global accepted principles. The Transpersonal leader moves from the ego and the local context to the global one. He considers local and regional contexts as just the starting points of his or her activities, and that he or she needs to think of the planet and the consequences of his or her actions on it. A question is necessary at this moment: what is socially acceptable, and who defines it? We believe that transpersonal leaders should initiate, in national and international venues, the discussion to define unnegotiable global values, ethical and moral principles that are inherent to humankind. This process, albeit long and complex, is necessary in order to establish a form of global agreement, which increases human beings' integrity in their local context, in their countries, and in broader international contexts. Which would be those non-negotiable principles for you? What principles would you include if you have the opportunity to advise leaders about universal ethical principles?

Facilitating moral and ethical standards development in others.

The Transpersonal leader is a promoter and facilitator of people's development. He or she conceives of others as potential leaders who need to move towards higher ethical and moral levels. Transpersonal leadership, in this sense, promotes learning through empowerment, active participation, reflection on personal performance, and metacognition – the awareness of understanding our thoughts and our knowledge-processes.

Empowerment is a fundamental process in transpersonal leadership. It gives people the ability to influence and decide. As we have established before, empowerment is giving power to the people and understanding that the best power is one that is widely distributed in all of us. Empowerment allows people to decide, change, and take new directions for their lives. Indeed, we believe that the promotion of active participation is fundamental in the leadership process. Promoting participation means to encourage supporters to become participants in the processes of change so they move from contemplation to belongingness, from disengagement to connection, and from inaction to action.

Transpersonal leadership promotes active participation because it is fundamentally democratic. Consequently, transpersonal leaders see democracy as the unique and most desirable socio-political contract to facilitate people's development and well-being. They focus on dissimilar points of view on the same subject and search for consensus to resolve differences, using ethics and morals, and social and global well-being as guiding principles.

Transpersonal leadership and democracy are aligned. The latter requires a legitimate leader with local, regional and global legitimacy. At the same time, global legitimacy requires collaborators and leaders who accept principles and values that transcend local barriers and move towards a universal context. Legitimacy in Transpersonal leadership does not relate to political processes, such as elections and selections in regional and international organizations, but to the ultimate and most valuable goal of leadership: attaining all's well-being through ethical and moral "performance". When this premise is included, leadership acquires a human and universal dimension. Within this scheme, it is impossible to catalog Hitler as a leader.

Transpersonal leadership combines different conceptions of leadership (attributes, situational, behavior-related, symbolic, moral, servant, and transformational) to develop people in all their facets. Developing people has to do with increasing their competencies in specific areas of knowledge, with the instilment of prosocial attitudes, and with the confidence that they have the capacities to promote their own development. A Transpersonal leadership vision should include in its wording the rising of people towards higher levels of personal consciousness and ethical and moral development based on knowledge and on practicing positive-social principles.

Transpersonal leaders accept that there may be more than one leader in a given situation - leadership can be shared - and each of them can lead in his or her areas of knowledge, and that leading and influencing depend on events' time, location, and contextual characteristics. Transpersonal leadership moves leadership from permanent power possession toward contextual-dependent-power. The Transpersonal leader understands leadership as a personal-social process where individuals, groups, organizations, societies, and hopefully the planet, should reach the highest level of ethical and moral development, and where any person can take a leadership role if he or she is more competent to do so.

Including themselves, the collaborators, and the context in decision-making and changing processes.

Leaders, collaborators, and their contexts affect each other in the leadership process. Transpersonal leaders and collaborators influence one another mutually. Additionally, they know that decision-making and change processes relate to the context, they change the context and the context models them. Transpersonal leaders understand that promoting or hindering change and decision-making may have lasting desirable or undesirable social consequences on people and on their environments. They understand that promoting changes without taking into account all the elements involved in a situation – the leader, the collaborators, and the context - reduces the possibility of changes' implementation and success.

In this sense, the transpersonal leader should have a holistic attitude when planning and when applying changes. In other words, transpersonal leaders need to understand the close interdependence among different social, technical, political, personal, cultural elements that affect leadership in multiple ways. Additionally, the transpersonal leader needs to consider each individual, institution, and social entity, as systems, and needs to know that particularities and interdependencies can affect positively or negatively - promote or hinder - the changes within these systems. The transpersonal leader should assess all these possible relationships between constituents before making decisions and proposing and implementing changes. Do you think that most of our leaders have a systemic or holistic view of social events?

Moving people from the use of external incentives toward the using of internal motivators.

Transpersonal leaders identify their needs. They know their motivations. They are internally motivated. This internal motivation is the generator of their behaviors. Additionally, transpersonal leaders, using the words of McClelland, are highly motivated by achievement, by doing things right, and by being successful. They undertake actions without seeking recognition. Recognition is not a motivating source; their motivating source is the need to do the best for the organization, the society, and the people. They believe the most genuine motives are people's social well-being. They carry out actions to facilitate social well-being and recognize that it is a motivating element in itself. Transpersonal leaders also recognize that many of their needs are satisfied by and through other people.

The Transpersonal leader is aware of his or her collaborators' motives. He or she knows that their motives can be associated with concrete rewards such as salary, position, social recognition, among others; nevertheless, he or she looks for common higher order motivators – ideas, ethical development, excellence, achievement, altruism, and solidarity, among others - to move people altogether in the same direction, toward a positive social development. He or she also recognizes that the needs of collaborators can be satisfied through external incentives but, progressively, substitutes these needs with social-high-order motivators to help develop self-motivation based on socially desirable performance and achievement. The transpersonal leader wants their collaborators to become social, ethical and moral leaders, just like him or her.

The transpersonal leader combines internal and external motives to promote and help collaborators achieve personal and work-related development. He or she knows that effective work is linked to collaborators' individual, organizational and social needs. He or she helps people to be aware that leadership development mixes internally controlled responsibility with the drive to serve others. The transpersonal leader is co-responsible for employees' development. Although transpersonal leaders understand that everyone has to learn to do things on their own, they also know that he or she is responsible for facilitating the conditions people need to perform their best in their contexts.

Moving from "the ego" towards the organization and the society, combining personal, organizational, social, and global knowledge

Transpersonal leaders think in a global organization/society. They understand that leadership development implies moving from the self to the organization, to the local community, to the global society. However, what makes leaders transpersonal is the consciousness that they must learn to lead themselves and their local context before attempting to take the lead of broader contexts.

Many so-called leaders who occupy "leadership" positions in their countries, for example, presidents, move to broader contexts, for example, international organizations, and are unable to do an effective job. The same happens in organizations when, excellent salespersons, for example, are promoted to managerial positions and are unable to perform as they used to. It happens to great professors who become department chairs and are unable to do their work. We think that many of them, although not leaders in their countries, work units, or classrooms did not know their strengths and limitations, were not aware of the required new competencies in the new environment, and maybe, did not know how the particularities of these new environments. They may not have known their new collaborators "agendas" and customs. They were not aware of the need to adopt new leadership behaviors. In the end, they were unable to lead people in those new environments.

Transpersonal leader who know themselves determine their own strengths, potentialities, and needs for development and knows how these characteristics affect their leadership skills. They are aware of their personal characteristics and use those that are positive while avoiding the use of those that are negative. They think deeply about their performance and ask others about it. They use 360-degree assessments, personality inventories and self-knowledge instruments to know which attitudes and behaviors are appropriate and why. In addition, transpersonal leaders think permanently about their actions. That is, they think deeply about the whys of their doings: why they behaved as they did in a given circumstance, why others reacted as they did it, what they failed to do, and which behaviors produced an inappropriate reaction in their collaborators. In other words, transpersonal leaders continuously reflect on their actions to reinforce socially positive behaviors and to change negative ones.

The second essential element of transpersonal leadership is the knowledge of the organization and society where the leader operates. Leaders should know organizational and social cultures, their members' motivations, and their characteristics to develop a high-achievement and people-wellbeing- service-oriented organization. In addition, they promote an organizational philosophy and culture, creeds, beliefs, and customs addressed to increase social-organizational development, and to transform or eliminate factors impeding the organizational development. The transpersonal leader knows members' creeds and ideas within the organization. He or she understands why they behave the way they do and uses this understanding to overcome individual differences that may work against organizational growth. He or she knows that people play the most important role in the construction of a positive organizational environment.

Transpersonal leaders understand that one of their key functions is to achieve the greatest benefit for everybody. However, they know that people, groups, and organizations benefits should be unquestionably accompanied by broad social achievements. Organizational benefits should be obtained without undermining the physical and social environment surrounding the organization.

Providing and promoting the creation of "significant" meanings in collaborators.

Providing and promoting the creation of "significant" meanings in collaborators happens when transpersonal leaders communicate to people the what, where, why, and when of an action. In this sense, they move from providing information and ideas to facilitating the interpretation of ideas, and then to the provision of ways to take actions. Transpersonal leaders believe that people want and need to know further than the 'what' is. Particularly, people need to know why they have to do what is asked for them to do. The transpersonal leader communicates and makes sure that collaborators understand the information, their ideas, and share the meaning of their vision.

Transpersonal leaders provide "significant meanings," meanings that make sense to people. They actively help people share those meanings by providing information and knowledge and by sharing with them the know-how, the "how to do meaning," so altogether be able to achieve their mission, and lately the organizational vision. They facilitate the use of previous information to adapt existing ways and create new ways to implement ideas, behaviors, and actions; this is the meaning of creativity. They establish, with collaborators, benchmarks and achievement standards, the "meaning of quality." In addition, the transpersonal leader encourages their supporters to use their ability to assess implementation and attainments, the "meaning of assessment." Transpersonal leaders and their collaborators develop the answers to questions related to where, why, how, when, and what is appropriate, through a democratic process. They accept everybody's participation, even of those who are slightly related to the issue or situation being discussed. They use ethics and morals, globally defined, as guiding principles to develop plural-pro-social actions. This is the meaning of communication within the transpersonal leadership framework.

In previous paragraphs, we have described the transpersonal leadership, a notion of leadership that goes beyond the simple ability to influence others to achieve results by using them. This conception of leadership includes influencing and being influenced by collaborators and achieving with others not by "using" others.

A final reflection. Think about your organization, community, country, or about the global context. Whom would you catalog as transpersonal leaders?

Summary

Transpersonal leadership is a process whereby the leader actively promotes the learning of his or her collaborators so that all of them reach social and globally shared purposes, leading to personal, organizational, social and global well-being.

Transpersonal Leaders:

1. Believe that people should become leaders of themselves and of others, guided by moral and ethical elements and by global and social principles that produce well-being for all.
2. Promote the development of others so they move towards higher levels of personal and social development.
3. Move from power to influence and make decisions towards a multi-directional inter-dependence leader, collaborator, and context to make decisions.
4. Move from using external motivational factors as main people's incentives toward understanding people's internal motivations. The leader encourages growth and change but, at the same time, recognizes that during this process, the collaborators can promote their own development.

The transpersonal leader knows that people are what their fellow human beings, communities, and societies do for them, and what people do for themselves.

Transpersonal Leadership

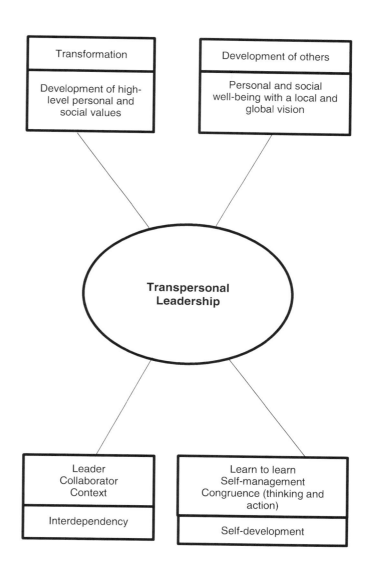

"The Transpersonal leader transcends his or her self, and lets a social-global legacy that endures over time and marks significantly the humanity."

Antonio Nicolás Rubino
Manuela Amat

8. Transpersonal leadership in the organizational context

We believe that management and leadership are two different organizational processes, and that transpersonal leadership is the type of leadership leaders should practice in organizations. These two premises move us to include this section. We use the steps of the ladder to transpersonal leadership as a frame of reference to describe and compare management and leadership in organizations. However, we want to show some previous comparisons that differentiate managers from leaders, a discussion that has been around for some years.

McFarland, I., Senn, I., and Childress, J. (1997) make a distinction between management and leadership. We summarize it into three groups: power and control, task orientation, and work relationships.

Management	Leadership
Power and Control	
• Acts like a boss • Exercises control and authority • Promotes centralization • Directs with rules and regulations • Establishes power hierarchies • Develops obedience	• Acts as a facilitator • Empowers • Distributes leadership and authority • Guides with shared values • Develops power based on relationships • Develops commitment
Task orientation	
• Focuses on individual or group goals • Focuses on the tasks and the figures • Change because of a crisis or a need	• Focuses on the organizational vision and strategy • Focuses on service to the receiver • Promotes learning and innovation

Work relationships	
• Confronts and competes • Makes emphasis on independence • Prefers networks of friends and acquaintances • Stimulates the competitiveness within the organization • Focuses on self, his or her unit, and the organization	• Collaborates and unifies • Makes emphasis on interdependence • Respects, honors, and supports diversity • Stimulates the global competitiveness in and out the organization • Focuses on the organization, the community, the society, the world

Management relates to the exercise of legitimate power, and to upholding the control in the organization, so the organization operates efficiently. Organizational tasks derive from pre-established objectives that must be achieved, and whose achievement defines the success or failure of the organization. Management sees the organization as an aggregate of separate units, where each must do its best and be efficient in its processes and particular results.

Leadership, on the other hand, is a relational process in which the power is distributed, and the leader does not instruct but rather promotes engagement as a form of self-regulation among collaborators. Likewise, leadership focuses on the organizational strategic elements that must provide the best service. The leader understands that an organization's performance and service should improve continuously. Finally, leaders see interdependence as a key element of the organizational structure where all internal and external organizational systems are connected.

Kotter (2005) made the distinction between management and leadership in relation to some of organizational activities and processes, which include planning, organizing, conflict control and resolution, and results. He pointed out:

Management	Leadership
Planning	
• Establishes the steps and time to achieve results. • Distributes resources to ensure the achievement of results.	• Develops a vision for the future. • Develops strategies to achieve the vision.
Organizing	
• Creates structures to achieve the plans. • Distributes staff. • Delegates in some people. • Creates policies and procedures to guide staff. • Creates monitoring and control systems.	• Communicates the direction of the organization. • Promotes collaboration and cooperation. • Promotes coalitions and teams to implement the strategies. • Promotes organizational vision and strategy acceptance.
Problems' control and resolution	
• Monitors results. • Identifies and corrects deviations from plans.	• Motivates and inspires people to overcome present or potential problems. • Promotes self-assessment. • Promotes changes to solve new situations.
Results	
• Focuses in the prediction and the order to produce organization stakeholders' expected results (customers, shareholders, employees, etc.).	• Produces changes and new ways to responding, suitable for those interested in the organization.

Management, according to Kotter, relates to tactical-operational aspects and leadership to strategic aspects. In other words, leaders have an organization holistic view and operate in a broader environment than managers do. Managers see the organization in a local context and are oriented toward an organization's short and medium-term goals. Managers are concentrated in everyday tasks. The leader focuses on a long-term vision. Some questions that people always ask us: who is better for the organization? Who is more important for the organization? Should we develop leaders or managers?

We believe that there are no simple answers to these questions. An organization needs good managers who keep it operating properly, within parameters of efficiency that would enable it to produce goods and services to please its customers. However, in volatile environments, such as the current one, it seems that having a vision or idea of permanent change is necessary. It is required to look beyond the obvious and to position the organization in future years and contexts. This is a leader's job rather than a manager job. Organizations need excellent managers to ensure their everyday functioning and need excellent transpersonal leaders who make organizations "dream" and do better even if they are already excelling. For us, a natural form of developing people in the organization is to move from management to leadership gradually, and to move from tactical roles to strategic roles after understanding the organization and its processes. Although this seems natural to us, it does not always happen in this way. Sometimes, a person who has not held management positions led the organization properly. However, we believe that the gradual development is the most appropriate and reasonable manner.

The Leadership ladder: Transpersonal Leadership in context

The differences between management and leadership established by McFarland and associates and Kotter apply to the stages of transpersonal leadership development. Additionally, these stages relate to management and leadership in different ways. The following views about transpersonal leadership, management, and leadership are based on people's opinions - from international universities, especially from the Caribbean, Central and South America, from manufacturing companies, from insurance companies, and from service organizations personnel, among others - who participated in leadership workshops. While reading, keep in mind the stages of transpersonal leadership development: *influencing people, influencing through socially acceptable ethical principles, facilitating personal and organizational development, practicing a socio-centered attitude, and practicing a global and ecological orientation.*

In the first step, we presented the process of influencing people and the forms of influence. The forms of influence that characterize management and leadership follow:

Management	Leadership
• Rational persuasion • Ingratiation • Personal connection • Transaction • Pressure	• Rational persuasion • Idealistic persuasion • Consulting • Coalition

In the second step, influencing through socially acceptable ethical principles, we found some the types of power that managers use more frequently than leaders. These include:

Management	Leadership
• Legitimate / formal • Reward/coercive • Possession of information	• Expert • Reference • Possession of information

The third step, facilitating personal and organizational development, includes several processes for people development. These processes relate to management and others to leadership in the following way:

Management	Leadership
• Delegating • Training	• Empowerment • Education and development • Shared decision making

In the next stage, practicing a socio-centered attitude, we found that the types of organizations and societies relate to leadership as follows:

Management	Leadership
• Prescriptive organizations	• Entrepreneur organizations • Knowledge organizations

Management seems to work better in prescriptive organizations while leadership does so in entrepreneurs and knowledge organizations.

Finally, the actions associated with the higher stage of transpersonal leadership, practicing a global and ecological orientation, should be associated with management and leadership. From our point of view and from the point of view of most participants, leaders and managers should:

- Value diversity and global empathy.
- Look for people and social well-being.
- Promote personal independence and social interdependence.
- Search for relationships within your organization and outside the organization.

Transpersonal Leaders, as established before, manage their own development while facilitating the development of others. They act keeping in mind people's characteristics and contextual elements, they move from their "egos" to the organization, the society and the world. They provide significant meanings to their collaborators. In addition, they develop self-internal motivation and controls, at the time that recognize and use external incentives to move people in the direction of obtaining benefits for them, the organization and the society.

Summary

There are clear differences between management and leadership. Some of them include the following:

Management relates to the maintenance and controls so that the organization operates efficiently. While leadership is a relational process, where power is distributed among people and where consultation, instead of instruction, is used to make decisions. Leadership promotes commitment as a form of self-regulation and self-control.

Management relates to tactical-operational aspects and leadership to strategic issues.

Organizations need managers who keep them operating properly, effectively, enabling them to produce goods and services for internal and external customers. However, in volatile environments, such as the current, a future oriented and change vision is necessary.

The relationships among the transpersonal leadership ladder, management and leadership show that some forms of influence relate to management; these include rational persuasion, Ingratiation, personal connection, transaction, legitimation, and pressure. Others are associated with leadership; these include rational persuasion, idealistic persuasion, consultation and coalition. Indeed, there are differences between management and leadership in relation to the use of power, organizational development processes, and organization orientation.

"Remember the difference between a boss and a leader; a boss says 'Go!' - A leader says 'let's go!'"

E.M Kelly

"Management is efficiency in climbing the ladder of success; leadership determines whether the ladder is leaning against the right wall."

Stephen R. Covey

A Final note

We are convinced that leadership is something deeper than just commanding people. We believe leadership has a high ethical, moral and socio-global content.

A person is not a leader because someone, at any given time, provides him or her with power, because he or she has a position in an organization or social group, or because he or she is able to get people to do what he or she wants to. A person is a leader because a he or she pursues well-being for all, because he or she respects the actions, opinions, and viewpoints of others, and because he or she respects diversity.

Undoubtedly, leadership relates to influencing people. However, the simplistic consideration of influencing to define leadership - which so far has been used by many people, including politicians, managers, executives, and organizations - is limiting and gives leadership a connotation of commander-subaltern, chief-follower, boss-subordinate, which disrespects people who have the right to intervene in the making of decisions that affect them. Influence used by a transpersonal leader allows others to develop and become leaders, too. In transpersonal leadership, influence implies positive personal and social development for all, leaders and collaborators.

The main challenge now is to change our paradigm in relation to what we define as leadership. A new paradigm based on the search for the well-being of all and not the benefit of only one person, or of the leader's group, or country. We believe that a leader becomes transpersonal when he or she undertakes actions to produce s well-being for all. A transpersonal leader gets desirable social results by increasing everyone's chances to participate in the social processes they are interested.

Leaders embark their development towards the transpersonal leadership when they understand that they are part of the world, of a system that goes beyond their personal, group, local or regional context; and when they understand the effects of their behavior in any of those contexts. The leader develops transpersonal leadership when he or she has the ability to think holistically, globally and ecologically.

Global and Ecological thinking are ingredients that must be present to achieve transpersonal leadership. Additionally, transpersonal leaders links their actions to moral and ethical principles related to people's permanent well-being.

Therefore, based on our conception of leadership, many of the so-called leaders are not. It is possible to call them commanders, rulers, coordinators or managers but not transpersonal leaders. We believe that transpersonal leadership is fundamental in today's society because transpersonal leadership is closely linked to pro-social purposes, which allows the society to exist and to provide benefits for its members.

Transpersonal leadership has to do with the transcendence of the leader, with moving toward high stages of ethical and moral development. Transpersonal leaders leave a positive legacy to the humankind. This is why we think that Jesus, Gandhi, Mandela and Mother Teresa of Calcutta, among others, reached the Trans-personality; and this is why Castro, Chavez, Hitler, and Bin Laden did not.

The returning question is who defines what is ethical and morally desirable? We believe that there in not a unique answer for everyone. However, it is part of the work of transpersonal leaders to seek actively, in the broadest global dimension, which the answer is, and to promote and facilitate in other leaders the finding of the answer. We think transpersonal leaders should strive for ethical and moral global principles in the same way they have fought for economic globalization.

Perhaps now is a good time for you to think about two fundamental questions that we believe you can answer easily, in which step of the leadership development are some of the today's leaders of your country? In addition, who of those considered leaders by you are transpersonal leaders?

We believe a fable we learned several years ago in a workshop about leadership development could help you to find the answers. The person who narrated the fable called it "The Fable of the Wise Man and the Teens."

In a distant village, there was a wise man, who always had answers to problems and situations submitted to him. In an occasion, two teenagers, tired of hearing that the man always had the solutions, and moved by the mischievous character of the age, decided to trick him. Thus, they caught a bird and went by to ask the wise man whether the bird was alive or dead. While they were walking toward the wise man's house, one of them said, "If the wise man tells us that it is alive, I will squeeze it, and I will open my hand and let it fall dead. If the man answers that it was dead, I will open my hand and let it fly."

They were sure they would deceive the wise man. They arrived at the man's house and told him: "Wise man, you always have the correct answers for every question. Can you tell us whether the bird I am holding in my hand is alive or dead?"

The wise man, looking thoughtfully at them, after a short time said, "The answer is in your hand."

We believe that the answers to the questions we presented through this book, as well as your development as a transpersonal leader, are in your hands.

"If your actions inspire others to dream more, learn more, do more and become more, you are a leader."

John Quincy Adams

References

Amat, M. (2007). Leadership in Higher Education Institutios (Liderazgo en Instituciones de Educacion Superior0. Doctoral dissertation. Universidad Pedagogica Experimental Libertador. Caracas, Venezuela.

Bass, B. (1981). *Stogdill's Handbook of Leadership: A Survey of Theory Research*. Revised and expanded edition by Bernard M. Bass. Free Press: New York.

Bass, B. & Avolio, B. (1990). *The implication of transactional and transformational leadership for individual, team, and organizational development*. In W. Pasmore and R. W. Woodman (Eds.) vol. 4. Greenwich, CT: JAI Press.

Bass, B. & Avolio, B. (1994). *Improving organizational effectiveness through transformational leadership*. Thousand Oaks: CA. SAGE Publications.

Bass, B. & Steidlmeiner, P. (1998). *Ethics, character, and authentic transformational leadership*. Center for leadership studies, School of Management. Binghamton University, Binghamton, N.Y. 13902-6015. Revised 9/24/98

Beck L.G. (1994). Reclaiming educational administration as a caring profession. New York: Teachers College Press.

Bennis, W. y Nanus, B. (1985). *Leaders: the strategies for taking charge*. New York: Harpers & Row.

Blake, R. y Mouton, J. (1964). *The managerial grid*. Houston: Gulf Publishing.

Boatman, S. (1997). Students Leadership Development: Approaches, Methods, and Models (Management of Campus Activities Series). Columbia, SC: National Association for Campus Activities Educational Foundation.

Brown M. E. & Treviño, L. K. (2006). Ethical leadership: A review and future directions. The Leadership Quarterly. 17, 596-616.

Burns, J. M. (1978). *Leadership*. New York: Harper & Row.

Clark, K. E. & Clark, M. (1996). *Choosing to lead*. Greensboro, NC: Center for Creative Leadership.

Daniels, M. (2008). *Sombra, Yo y Espíritu. Ensayos de psicología transpersonal*. Kairós: Barcelona.

De Pree, M. (1989). *Leadership is an art*. A Dell Trade Paperback: New York.

Fiedler, F. E. (1967). *A Theory of Leadership Effectiveness*. New York: McGraw Hill.

Fiedler, F. E. & Chemers, M.M. (1985). *Liderazgo y administración efectiva*. México: Trillas.

French, J. y Raven, B. (1959). *The bases of social power*. In D. Cartwright (Ed.). Studies of social power. Ann Arbor, MI: Institute for Social Research.

Gasper, J. M. (1992). *Transformational leadership: an integrative review of the literature*. Ann Arbor, MI: U.M.I. Dissertation Information Service.

Green, R. (2001). *Practicing the Art of Leadership: a problem based approach to implementing the ISLLC standards*. Upper Saddle River, NJ: Merrill Prentice Hall Inc.

Grof, S. (2000). *La psicología del futuro. Lecciones de la investigación moderna de la consciencia*. Barcelona: La Liebre de Marzo.

Hackman, M. Z. & Johnson, C. E. (1991). *Leadership: a communication perspective*. Prospect Heights, ILL: Waveland Press Inc.

Hemphill, J. & Coons, A. (1957). *Development of leader behavior description questionnaire*. In R. Stogdill y A. Conos (Eds.). Leader behavior: Its description and measurement. Columbus, Ohio: Bureau of Business Research. Ohio State University.

Hersey, P. & Blanchart, K. (1982). *Management of organizational behavior: utilizing human resources*. Englewood Cliff, NJ: Prentice Hall, Inc.

Hitt, W. (1990). Ethics and Leadership: Putting Theory into Practice. Columbus: Battelle Press

Hodgkinson, C. (1991). *Educational Leadership: the Moral Art*. Albany, NY: State University of New York Press.

Jacobs T. & Jaques, E. (1990). *Military executive leadership*. En K. Clark y M. Clark (Eds.). Measures of leadership. West Orange, NJ: Leadership Library of America.

Katz, D. & Kahn, R. (1978). *The social psychology of organization* (2nd. Ed.) New York: John Wiley.

Kotter, J. (2005) Leading Change. Harvard Business School Press.

McFarland, L., Senn, L. & Childress, J. (1997). *Liderazgo para el siglo XXI. Diálogos con 100 líderes destacados.* Serie McGraw Hill Liderazgo en acción. Editorial McGraw Hill Interamericana, S.A. Colombia.

McClelland, D. (1985). *Human motivation*. Glenview, IL: Scott Foresman.

McGregor, B. (2003). *Transforming Leadership*. Grove Atlantic Inc., New York.

McGregor, D. (1960). *The human side of enterprise*. New York: McGraw-Hill.

Owens, R. (1998). *Organizational Behavior in Education.* Needham Heights, MA: Allyn and Bacon.

Pastin, M. (1984).Ethics as an integrating force in management. *Journal of Business and Ethics,* 3 (4), 293-304.

Rauch, C. y Behling, O. (1984). *Functionalism: Basis for an alternate approach to the study of leadership.* In J. Hunt, D. Hosking, C. Schriesheim, y R. Stewart (Eds.). Leaders and managers: International perspectives on managerial behavior and leadership. Elmsford, NY: Pergamon Press.

Rubino, A. (1990). Diseño y producción de cuestionarios para establecer los estilos de Liderazgo, la madurez del grupo, el poder del líder sobre los subordinados, la estructura de la tarea y las relaciones líder-subordinado: desde el punto de vista del líder y los subordinados. Trabajo de ascenso no publicado. Universidad Pedagógica Experimental Libertador, Instituto Pedagógico de Caracas, Caracas.

Rubino, A. (2001, Octubre). El Liderazgo transformacional: una forma de liderar efectivamente las organizaciones. Conferencia presentada en la Academia Militar de Venezuela, Caracas.

Rubino, A. & Amat, M. (2001). Atributos de los líderes (Leader's Attributes). Workshop materials.

Solomon, R. & Hanson, K. (1983).Above the Bottom Line: An Introduction to Business Ethics. New York: Harcourt Brace Jovanovich.

Sargent, J. F. & Miller, G. R. (1971). Some differences in certain communication behavior of autocratic and democratic group leaders. *Journal of Communication, 21,* 238-258

Stogdill, R. (1974). *Handbook of leadership-A survey of theory and research.* New York: The Free Press.

Tannenbaum, R., Wescheler, I. & Massarik, F. (1961). *Leadership and organization*. New York: McGraw-Hill.

Thiroux, J. & Krasemann, K. (2001). Ethics: Theory and Practice. Upper Saddle River, N.J. Prentice Hall.

Wilber, K. (1989). *El proyecto Atman. Una visión transpersonal del desarrollo humano*. Barcelona: Kairós.

Yukl, G. (1994). *Leadership in organizations*. (3rd. Ed.) New York: Prentice Hall.

Yura, H., Ozimek, D. & Walsh, M. (1976). *Nursing leadership: Theory and Process*. New York: Appleton-Century-Crofts.

Made in the USA
Middletown, DE
01 December 2018